Art by
Jeanette Sha

THIS IS COMPASSION!

British Columbia's youth (ages 12 to 18)

reflect on giving, receiving, witnessing, observing, listening, accepting, action, courage, hope & understanding compassion.

Published by the Stories of Compassion Project

ISBN: 978-0-9812721-0-8

Copyright © 2009
Stories of Compassion Project

Printed in Canada
Layout and design:

TruffleTree Publishing

Cover art
Helping hands
By Allison Brown
To show compassion through a piece of visual art, I chose a multi-media picture. All three figures are in black and white but the patterns are different, revealing different backgrounds and stories. The background is the warmest at the right-hand side, fading to the left, representing the figures' well-being and power in life and leaving the strongest person in the highest spot. Each figure is reaching out to the person below, creating a chain effect – helping one another to higher ground. It symbolizes that if you lend a hand to someone the same will be done for you in return.

Back cover
(From left to right)
Top row:
Shaylene Charleson
Rebecca Shaw
Lina Martin-Chan
Jocelyn Wong
Second row from top:
Gayle Oh
Sandra Fossella
Ella Moynihan
Becci Delacruz
Third row from top:
Lina Martin-Chan
Zahara Baugh
Becci Delacruz
Katrina Allison
Bottom row:
Joel Chern
Brenda De Vera
Alexa Engh
Nikita Morgan

The Stories of Compassion Project acknowledges the support of:

DALAI LAMA CENTER

FOR PEACE AND EDUCATION

Contents

Art (from top) by Cindy Lin, Carrie Ng and Coco Xiao

Art (from top) by Sachie Ricketts, Ji Eun Park and Lisa Xie

Nurturing Compassion

An Introduction by Maria LeRose

What would happen if you asked a high school student to tell a personal story about compassion? The cynics among us might say that young people today do not know the meaning of compassion. These individuals believe that in this fast-paced, competitive world teenagers have become self absorbed, and have no interest in others. I am happy to report that these cynics would be wrong.

In 2006 teachers from Coast Metro secondary schools invited their students to write a story about a personal experience with compassion. The students were told that in September 2006 the Dalai Lama would be visiting Vancouver and that a selection of their stories would be presented to him. The response was overwhelming. Hundreds of students openly shared stories about experiences that changed their lives – and made them more compassionate. There were stories about the environment, pets, friends, family and chance encounters with strangers. Some were painful, others happy. But all of the stories were written from the heart.

Nine students aged 13 to 17 were selected to share the stage with the Dalai Lama and engage him in a dialogue entitled *Nurturing Compassion*. The event would also be broadcast around the world via the internet. Supported by adult mentors, including myself, the students spent the summer months preparing for the dialogue.

They spent time writing, researching and rehearsing.

The most important preparation involved their personal reading and reflections about compassion in their lives. This was their chance to prepare their minds and hearts for an extraordinary experience. The students came from a variety of cultural and religious backgrounds. One of the things they had in common: a commitment to make this dialogue meaningful, not only for themselves, but for all the youth and adults attending the event. And, of course, they wanted to engage the Dalai Lama in an authentic conversation and learn from his reflections.

The students each took on specific roles. Two of them volunteered to be MCs, writing their own script and setting the tone for this special dialogue. Another student was the moderator. She guided the flow of the dialogue by directing questions and facilitating follow-up conversations. Three students shared their stories through short films. And all of them had the opportunity to ask the Dalai Lama a question. On September 8th, 2006, the students stepped onto the stage of the Orpheum Theatre in front of thousands of people – and watched with awe and excitement as the Dalai Lama entered the room. In the introductory comments the student MCs said:

We, as youth, are the next generation of global citizens; the question is what type of global citizens we choose to be. Today is an opportunity to talk about important values that will help us make the world a better place. One such value is compassion.

The students spent only three hours with the Dalai Lama – a very short time in the span of their lives. But these three hours will be forever etched in their memories and their hearts. One of them returned to school after the dialogue and immediately wrote down his thoughts about the experience:

No matter what colour, age or religion, we are beings born with seeds of compassion planted deep within our hearts. We are creatures who can't fully thrive unless we have empathy and truth in our lives. But it is up to us to cultivate those seeds of compassion, giving them sunshine and attention, solid ground and stability, and every now and then, a little darkness and rain. After all, if there was no suffering in the first place, there wouldn't be anything to be compassionate about. In the end, we must nurture our hearts with love, because before we can begin to better the world around us, we must first begin with bettering ourselves.

What did I learn from this experience? We need to provide opportunities for young people to experience and talk about compassion, altruism and empathy. Not only are they capable of this level of discourse – it is the very thing that will help build resilience in their lives.

Art by Alexa Engh

Continuing the Conversation

A Preface by Susanne Martin

The Dalai Lama's dialogue with high school students in 2006 was the catalyst for starting a conversation with British Columbia's youth – a conversation about compassion. The students had been invited to submit stories about their experience with compassion and the results were astounding. The organizers of the event came to the conclusion that the conversation should not come to an end when the Dalai Lama left the city. With the support of Frog Hollow Neighbourhood House, the Vancouver School Board and the Dalai Lama Center for Peace and Education, the Stories of Compassion Project was initiated with the mandate to continue the conversation as well as make the stories available to a general audience.

The Stories of Compassion Project received over 300 entries of stories and artwork from 38 public and independent schools in British Columbia. All the entries are meaningful, even if they haven't found a place in the following pages. There are many examples of the Stories of Compassion Project in action. A Box of Friendship, built by a grade nine student and submitted to the project, is displayed in the entrance hall of a school to remind everyone to get along and overcome bullying. After

researching and writing an essay on compassion, a grade eight student has decided to go to Mexico and volunteer for the "Housing for Humanity" project to help people who live in poverty. And in an unusually quiet grade-seven classroom, a student had finished reading her compassion story when a friend broke the silence with a whispered remark, "Look, Mr. C. (vice-principal and humanities teacher) is crying."

Writing about compassion, creating a piece of art or taking a photo about the subject, is not as easy as it sounds. Compassion is not a common school-yard topic and several students started by looking up the definition in the dictionary. But from there, they went in different directions. They remembered incidents of compassion they had witnessed, heard about or experienced. It seems that the students found compassion almost everywhere. By actively looking for compassion, they invited it into their lives and were able to share it with others through their creative work. With this book, they will be able to reach a wider audience. But it should not be viewed as an end result but rather as a stepping stone in an ongoing conversation about compassion.

Art by Colin Ruloff

Understanding

Angela Tsui

Pizza Boxes and Changing the World

A month ago I attended a model United Nations conference. I was excited at first. I was going to be a part of something huge. I was going to sit down with young intellectuals like myself and discuss ideas on how to spread love in the world, to change the world, to save the world, to bring world peace. I was a naïve, bumbling girl floating on pink clouds.

The experience was life-altering, but not in the way I expected it to be. What struck me hardest was the inability of the model UN to solve anything. There were debates. Yes, there were endless debates. Debates on which topic to debate first and debates on whether or not to debate at all. It was an endless cycle of debates. I spoke, motioning for less radical movements other than declaring war, which some of the stronger debaters kept motioning for, but I felt my words fall on deaf ears, and my confidence abandoned me. Everyone only cared about presenting their ideas. Not many listened. Still fewer cooperated. I realized that I was not so different. My messages became empty, hollow, devoid of meaning. Something in me died.

We had pizza for dinner. Boxes upon boxes of pizza, all piled up. They were everywhere. At the end of the conference, those boxes, some still filled with pizza, were ditched into the garbage or stuffed into abandoned corners. The next morning, I came across a small, crooked old man sorting through the pizza boxes in front of the cafeteria. I stopped. He was opening the boxes, shaking his head, putting them in neat stacks apart from the rest of the usual garbage. He looked at me, saw my dress and pressed shirt. And I will always remember that funny, sad smirk. "Trying to change the world," he began, and shook his head, "when you can't even recycle! There's food in some of these boxes yet. People are starving out there, the environment needs protecting, and you, model UN,

you can't bother to look through the boxes, to put them in the right place. You are trying to save the world when you couldn't even save yourself."

I discovered that the wisest thing anyone said at model UN came from a school janitor. Something terrible happened: I lost hope. My pink clouds vanished. I lost hope in compassion, I lost hope in democracy. I lost hope in the spirit of mankind. When I got home, I sat at the dinner table and cried. My father found me like this and I told him what had happened. I told him about my frustration and anger at the other delegates, my utter helplessness at what people do to those around them, like that poor janitor. He looked at me and said softly, "You may feel that there is no compassion, no hope in the world, but remember, there is always forgiveness."

Forgiveness, I thought. At one in the morning, I sat in the kitchen, and I thought about forgiveness. I forgave myself for not fighting hard enough for my ideas. I forgave the students for being competitive. I forgave the janitor for feeling frustrated. I forgave the world for all its conflict. Everyone has reasons for their actions. If you can't do anything to stop it, accept it, and forgive. For you see, it is only through forgiveness that you can find peace, and through peace, understanding, and with understanding, calm. And it is only with calm that you can approach the matter at hand in a rational manner with no frustration, no anger and no hatred. In the wake of the conference, I have made forgiveness a mental process that comes from my soul. It seems sincere that way. How do I affect others? Not much, but somewhere deep down, every time someone crashes into me in the hall, or someone says something cruel, I will accept them, and forgive them. And in my own little way I can contribute to the vast realm that is human compassion.

Stephen Boles

Free Lunch

According to the dictionary, compassion is "a deep aware-ness of the suffering of another coupled with the wish to relieve it." So must someone be in trouble or sad in order to be shown compassion? This story shows how compassion brought two friends together.

September 2004, grade nine humanities. I remember it as if it were yesterday. There was a boy called Kevin* in my class who sat right in front of me. Kevin had autism. I will admit that I did make fun of him at first. But one day he approached me and we talked about every possible topic – from girls to video games. After class his teacher assistant asked if I would like to spend one lunch a week with him and in return, I would receive one free lunch per week. I agreed instantly. Why not a free lunch? The next week I shared one lunch hour with Kevin and I actually had a good time. The next week I decided to go twice. I still had a great time and I did collect my free lunch. I'm a teen; who wouldn't take advan-tage of that at my age?

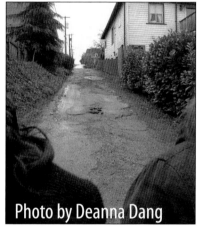
Photo by Deanna Dang

But then I started thinking: why? Why would I take a free lunch as payment for having a great time? So the next week, I went to sit with Kevin every day and had a blast even without a free lunch. A couple of weeks passed and I decided to bring along another friend. He had just as much fun as I did. At lunch we would always stay in one room just talking.

One day Kevin decided to go for a walk in the hall. This was a big step. He usually didn't like to walk in crowded areas. So we ate in the room and then the three of us went for a walk. There is something I forgot to tell you about Kevin. As someone with autism, Kevin is a slave to routine. Unless his day is planned down to the exact minute, he has a bad day and sometimes takes it out on everyone. So going for a walk was a big step in a good direction.

A few months later, I suggested to Kevin that we might buy our lunch at the cafeteria and eat it there too. He refused. I dropped the subject until one day he brought his money to school. I was very surprised. I walked with him to the cafeteria and he bought an ice cream sandwich, two cookies and a large chocolate milk. Probably not the healthiest lunch, but what the heck, it was his first time at the cafeteria.

Months passed and Kevin would occasionally buy his lunch be-cause he had gained confidence from his first experience. In the last couple of weeks at school, Kevin started at-tending only half days so we couldn't spend lunch together. I went to see him at break instead and we hung out for those 15 minutes. The time just flew by. In the summer we drifted apart and I thought to myself, there is always next year. But Kevin moved and started going to another school. I have seen him only once this year, at the mall. We talked for half an hour and then we said our good-byes and left. What Kevin doesn't know is that I cherished my time with him no matter what his mood was or what others thought. He taught me so much. And I wish to have a chance to thank him for it.

* not his real name

Veronyca Trebesh
Belated Thank You

Having heart surgery doesn't happen to anyone – especially not when they're only three and a half years old. I was born in 1990 in the Ukraine to parents who weren't very well off. The first day after my birth, it was obvious that something needed to be done. Only three chambers of my heart were functioning, and two big holes were causing my blood to mix and my appearance to be somewhat 'blue'. I wasn't a normal three-year-old. I couldn't run or even walk very far without being overwhelmingly tired. Since I had an older brother, my parents could see that something was very wrong. But they would never have been able to afford the surgery that would enable me to survive past the age of ten.

How could my parents save me? They searched frantically for a way to help their second child and only daughter. Finally, a friend living in the US arranged for me to have surgery. At the age of three years, I flew to America to receive the most generous gift of my life. I met Rodolfo Neirotti. He was living and breathing compassion, it seemed. He was a very skilled surgeon who agreed to operate on me, free of charge, giving up a pay-cheque of US$50,000. After the successful surgery, my doctor asked me for a simple kiss on the cheek, for thanks. Since I was only three years old, I firmly shook my head and said, "No" in Russian. He smiled none the less and wished me luck.

Many years later, as I look back on those days, I realize that I hardly knew what was happening. I would thank everyone in that hospital, tenfold. I would thank everyone who worked so hard to make that surgery happen. Compassion is much more than what any old dictionary says. One person's compassion can change everything. One person's compassion changed my life. I hardly even thanked him. There will always be a time when I will ask, "Why me?" or "What did I do?" But now I realize that without Dr. Neroti, I wouldn't be able to ask those questions.

I was a silly little girl who should have thanked him with her whole heart, as I do now every day. If it wasn't for compassion, I wouldn't be here, telling this story. If it wasn't for the people who love me and care for me, I wouldn't be here, living as a normal teenager. Compassion saved my life. It seems it can do anything. What will it do next?

The Source

Art by Katrina Allison

When I thought about compassion I considered where it comes from, which is the heart. I displayed this in my piece by showing a man holding his hands over his heart, his source of compassion.

Andrina Fawcett

A Stranger's Kindness

There are moments in life, so precious and rare that we hold them tightly and close to our hearts in hopes that we too will be able to pass on moments of compassion to another.

As young children, our view of the world is small – our whole universe consists of a few blocks stretching outwards from our home. We lack the worldly views attained as we grow older, and many times, because of this, we do not understand the magnitude of the acts of kindness shared with us. For a long while, I contemplated what I should write for this opportunity. I spent much time researching the Dalai Lama and his works in hopes that I could further understand the concept of compassion. When reading about a deep awareness of suffering coupled with a wish to relieve it, I realised that the most powerful piece I could write would be a personal one.

I must have been eight or nine years old, sitting out on the hard, cold cement. There had been an argument with two of my friends and I was distraught and angry. They had left me there, curled up, my face buried in my knees. In retrospect, it was such a trivial matter, but at the time, the issue was all encompassing, and I was sure that my friends could never be forgiven. I sat a long while, in tears, unsure of what to do. It was towards the end of summer, late August and the sunlight was fleeting. A cool evening breeze had started, yet I remained on the cement, my knees held close to my torso. In these last few moments before nightfall, I experienced my first true moment of compassion.

She came from down the street, arms cradling something inside her coat. My sobs, which

moments ago had echoed up and down the boulevard, were now hushed as this odd person appeared. Although she was across the street, she paused observing me in my huddled state, and took the time to cross over. No words were spoken as she came and sat down next to me on the pavement. I was alarmed to say the least, but I remained seated. Reaching inside her coat, she brought out what she had been cradling: a tiny puppy. It was small and grey, eyes not yet open, so innocent and fragile. She placed the little puppy in my waiting arms. Something so innocent and fragile can shock you into a different frame of mind. You wonder if anything so small and defenseless can survive. The troubles of moments before melted into insignificance in the presence of this small being.

Eventually she asked me what it was that had upset me, and she gave me the option not to answer. In some ways I felt ashamed for being so distraught over such a small matter, so I told her it was nothing. She sat with me until nightfall, when I heard the call of my mother, beckoning me home. I gave her back the little puppy, passing it to her with great care. She slipped it back inside her coat, cradling it once again. I arose and said goodbye. She smiled and waved as she turned to leave. I ran towards the lights of home.

Years later, I am still moved by the anonymous person's act of compassion. Although I did not understand the significance of her actions at the time, she helped me gain a more balanced view, and for that I thank her greatly. It remains in my mind as one of those few precious moments in life that I will forever hold dear, and aspire to.

Sean Meadows

Grandfather's Wisdom

October 8, 2005. Under the severe influence of alcohol and stress, my father threatened to kill my mother and my brother with a five-foot steel pole. That night, my father had to spend a night in jail and had a restraining order put on him so he could not come within one block of my family and my house.

This is where my most powerful personal experience of empathy and compassion comes in. The next day, my grandfather (my mom's dad) actually went and talked to my father trying to guide him through his alcoholic problem. I, for one, wanted to kill my dad for what he put my family through that night. But not my grandpa. He actually had empathy and compassion for the man who had threatened to kill his daughter and grandson. My grandfather told me that his intention of going over to see my father was not to yell at him or hurt him. It was to make him understand that he needed help and give him the support to do so.

When my grandfather explained this to me, I learned that even though my father put me and my family though a lot of pain, we should not be like him and repay him with pain. Instead, we needed to give him support so he could seek help and break the cycle of causing pain to others and to himself.

Art by Kira Martin-Chan

For the compassion project I decided that I wanted to draw a picture of hands. When I think of compassion and hands I automatically think of the peace symbol. I wanted to do something original. The night before I drew this picture, I watched *Peter Pan*. I was inspired by the movie because in the beginning Peter Pan goes into Wendy's room looking for his shadow. This was how I came up with the idea of an action and the shadow being different: revealing what you are underneath it all. The fist in the picture represents anger, hate, spite, and violence. Compassion is represented by the shadow of a hand in the shape of a peace symbol. The message of my picture is that you may seem violent but everyone has a compassionate side.

Charles Huang

The Assault

These past few months, I feel like I have been spiraling into a chasm. I try to clamber my way back out, yet I meet new confrontations every day. Life is all about experience and by familiarizing yourself with all kinds of danger, risks, menaces and threats, you will become stronger. By not giving up, I know that one day I can look back at the abyss with a smile on my face.

My story started a few months ago when I was on a bus riding home on a crisp February night. After I had got off the bus and crossed the street, three men jumped on me and started pummeling my face and my body. They sent me sprawling onto the ground and didn't give me a chance to cry out. After a minute of squirming, I managed to crawl a few steps. Suddenly I noticed a gleam of moonlight reflected on a blade held in front of my face. It was then that I froze. They took my jacket and my bag that held my court shoes, change of clothes, wallet and mp3. Even after they ran away, I still couldn't move. Finally, I bolted home and phoned the police. The three men were never found and my belongings were never returned.

The possibility of finding the offenders was slim. I tried my best to identify them but it had been too dark to see their faces. Again and again, the police questioned me about possible suspects and I had to respond with the same identifications. Truly, I wanted the three men to be arrested – not because I wanted my belongings back or because I wanted to see them punished, but rather because I wanted to know that they were off the streets and wouldn't attack a second, or third victim. Did I feel hate for them? Truthfully, yes, I did hate them. I was disgusted that three men would attack and rob a sixteen-year-old. Sympathy and support from my family and friends helped me pull through this incident.

Recently I had a heated argument with a team-mate on my ultimate team. He called me a back-stabber for helping the other team call a foul. Ultimate is a team sport that is self-refereed. When there is a dispute, the teams talk it out and then come to a decision together.

I was only trying to play a fair game. I urged my team-mate to stop complaining and concentrate on playing. He replied with a threat, "Are you trying to start something? One call and you're dead." It was then that the incident from the February night flooded back into my mind and my whole body started trembling with rage and fury. However, I backed away – I walked off my temper. Why did I not rush at him in a frenzy? I was not frightened of facing suspension, a black eye or a bleeding nose, but I did think about the consequences. If I had fought with him, he would later call his friends and try to harass me. I knew that if that happened, my friends would definitely jump in and help and I didn't want them to get involved. I also remember my older brother once telling me, "The person who throws the first punch loses." My brother was telling the absolute truth. The person who initiates the fight, automatically loses. And I would rather make a friend than a new enemy. Lastly, I would hate to see the expressions on my mother's and his mother's faces when they saw us coming home beaten and bruised. My team-mate and I haven't talked since.

Even though both of these incidents have not been fully resolved, my knowledge has been broadened and I attempted to change my dislike and hatred into empathy and compassion. From the robbers' point of view, I am almost certain that they must loathe themselves for attacking a sixteen-year-old. I also think that my team-mate regrets making those threats. For now I have not entirely forgiven them, but I'll try never to throw the first punch or give up. I know that I can overcome these incidents. Then one day I will be clear of the abyss. After all, the abyss is only the darkness and hate of one's mind.

Andrew Smith

Nothing is Promised

The dictionary's defines compassion as "a deep awareness of the suffering of another coupled with the wish to relieve it," but I think it goes deeper than that. Compassion can come from sympathy, empathy or just the goodness of one's heart. People don't generally show enough of it these days – or at least not until something happens to them to point the way.

My story of compassion is based on an experience with my youngest brother. I am not really sure why I always upset him, but I have come across an explanation. When I was younger, my middle brother and I were mistreated…well actually, we were abused by our dad, both physically and verbally. My youngest brother was not subject to this. He was just a baby, and therefore has no harsh memories of our father. But for my mom, my middle brother and me, the pain of the abuse has left deep wounds in our hearts. Eventually, my dad moved out. My brothers and I grew over the years, but the memories were still very much alive.

My brothers and I had become fairly wild kids. Having no man in the house to guide us, we were always out of control. About a year and a half ago, something seemed to have entered the minds of us two oldest boys. When we got stressed out from school or grappled with personal issues, we took it out on the youngest brother. It wasn't so bad at first but then it escalated to a point where we were calling him extremely harsh names. It seemed like an evil mentality had taken hold of us, I concluded, after asking myself many times why we behaved this way.

If you think about it, we were projecting the violent image of our dad. And to this day I still wonder whether our actions were a reflection of what he had done to us.

I knew that my actions hurt my youngest brother but I felt the need to take my anger and frustration about my life out on someone. And then I learned that he was much, much more upset than I had thought possible. My mom told me all the things he said to her. After she had told me everything, I was choked. I thought back on all the insults I had hurled at my brother. I understood that he is a smart, loving kid, but if he keeps being treated this way, he may think that something is wrong with him. And that's not right.

I waited a couple of days and then decided to talk to my brother about it. I told him how sorry I was. I have to say that he handled this more maturely than I would have in his position. He told me that I just needed to learn to control myself because he wanted the remaining years we are living in the same household to be happy ones. I'm really glad that my brother and I were able to talk about this. And I'm proud of him for finding it in him to forgive me for the living hell I put him through.

My brother and I spend a lot of time together now. We play board games and watch soccer matches. Sometimes we just hug, thankful that we have one another. My dad is getting a lot better too. My brother and I visit him every second weekend and we like spending time with him.

Nothing is promised but things are sure getting better.

Sandra Fossella

Kitchen Duty

Art by Asia McLean

When I was younger, my father would bring me to downtown East Vancouver where he did some things he felt he needed. I remember being a scared little child following my dad closely in fear somebody might try to harm me. I had this image of every person being evil because they were where they were. And they had grungy, dirty clothes that smelled of urine and sweat.

When I was at school and being raised by my grandparents, I would not see my father for days because he was downtown wandering the streets and committing crimes. I would worry about him because I knew that he would not eat and take proper care of himself.

My father decided to go into treatment when I was thirteen. The treatment centre was located in the middle of Skid Road where it was dirty, dark and smelly. When I went to see him, my thoughts consisted of "Oh my god, we have to be around a bunch of smelly people and see these addicts using all around us." But it wasn't like this.

At one time, when I was visiting my dad, he had to go and help in the kitchen. I decided to go with him and volunteer. I helped setting up for the meal, thinking it was for the other men in the treatment centre. But I found out that we were going to be serving food to homeless people and that made me happy. I was happy to hear that people with nowhere to go had a place to eat and keep warm. I felt warm inside when the people came to me with large smiles and I couldn't to see the usual pain in their eyes. My dad knew a few of the men and introduced me to some of his friends and I could see how proud he was of me. I have different thoughts about homeless people now. I'm not scared and I don't look down on them like many people in the world. I continue to volunteer in the kitchen every so often because I love the feeling it brings to the people as well as myself.

Christine Quintana

Tiny White Dog

One of our world's wisest men once said that "the greatness of a nation and its moral progress can be judged by the way its animals are treated" – and I believe Gandhi was right. In my 12 years of volunteering at the Vancouver SPCA, I have seen the very best and worst of human nature. I have been shocked by the capacity for cruelty, and touched by the dedication and love shown to our animal companions. But the greatest lessons in compassion have been taught to me by the animals themselves. In a world where some know nothing of tenderness or affection, these pets learn to forgive the human race and forget years of abuse and neglect in order to start anew. Time and time again as I watch abandoned or ill-treated dogs and cats become rehabilitated into loving and well-adjusted pets, I am inspired by their willingness to forgive and their ability to return the love and companionship shown to them. In a society where violence too often becomes the bottom line, we would be wise to look to our animal friends for the lessons of forgiveness and compassion we humans greatly need.

Over the years, my family and I have taken many abused or ill pets into our home in order to rehabilitate them and sometimes find them new homes. Being a 'foster parent' to an animal can be a heartbreaking experience, but it is always a rewarding one. Many animals that have come to us seemingly irreparably traumatized soon learned to trust and love again despite having faced appalling abuse at the hands of fellow human beings.

One such a case is Billy, a dog rescued from a puppy mill. Puppy mill dogs are kept for the sole purpose of breeding, and rarely, if ever, receive human contact. Instead, the animals are kept in tiny wire cages, isolated and malnourished, and killed when they no longer produce puppies. These animals are the victims of human greed, and when the authorities manage to find and rescue them, many are beyond help and are unable to be adopted. Billy was supposed to be such a case, but my family took on the challenge of helping this animal. We brought him home with us and were deeply saddened to see the extent of his emotional trauma. The tiny white dog would run repeatedly in a circle, approximately the size of the cage he used to call home. Upon seeing a human being approach, Billy would run and hide until he heard footsteps walking away. Having never known compassion from a human being, Billy was fearful and mistrusted us. But slowly, over the weeks and months, he learned what a loving home could be like. He learned from the friendship of our other dogs and the care shown to him by us. Every day, he would walk a little closer to us before running away, until one day, he came up and licked my hand – a gesture seemingly so small, yet so great in magnitude. After a lifetime of neglect and abuse, this animal had learned to trust again. I was touched by the bravery of this little dog.

It saddens me to know that there are people in our society who will intentionally harm another living creature. As a longtime volunteer at the SPCA, I have heard stories of unspeakable acts of violence committed against animals purely for sport and this frightens me. Anyone who is capable of such violence against an animal is surely capable of the same against a human being. Those who exploit animals for money also raise the question: Is compassion not truly the most valuable currency? I find it funny that the lessons taught to me by these animals can best be described as lessons in humanity.

In showing respect and empathy for all living creatures, they teach us the lessons our society needs the most – lessons of compassion and forgiveness, even in the face of violence and fear.

Ty Helgason

Jimmy

Gimme Shelter

Art by Zahara Baugh

My image is of a dog being sheltered from the rain and being given food. This image represents compassion because people are showing their concern for a starving, wet dog by feeding and sheltering it.

Jimmy was a dog in our community's SPCA. He had been adopted and returned to the SPCA three times. He was a smart, good-looking border collie but had separation anxiety: when he was left alone he went ballistic. The SPCA staff had tried many things to try to get him to calm down. Nothing would work and he was becoming a problem because every night someone had to take him home. If he was left there, he wrecked all the blinds in the building. If he was caged, he freaked out and hurt himself trying to break out of his cage. Nobody knew what to do. The SPCA staff had put up posters everywhere with Jimmy's picture but nobody was calling and they needed the space in the building. If no one were to adopt him, he would have to be put down.

The first family that had adopted him from the SPCA had brought him back because they had to work for just a few hours each day, but in that time Jimmy ripped up everything he could get his paws on. The second person brought him back for the same reason but the third just returned him because he did not want to pay for dog food and did not want to take care of him.

About two months after he was returned to the SPCA for the third time, a family wanted to adopt him. This time, the SPCA staff was cautious but the people assured them that Jimmy would never be alone. They had three kids who were between eight and fourteen, so there would always be someone around, except when they went out. But they promised that they would hire a babysitter for him for those occasions.

These people have looked after Jimmy for around a year and a half now and still have not returned him. So Jimmy ended up with the perfect family because the people at our SPCA, and a family that really wanted a dog, showed some patience and compassion.

Jenny Scott

Home Again

When I was sixteen, I left home to live with my boyfriend, Alex. We had fun going to parties and living the life I thought I wanted. Then one cold day in late September, I found out that I was pregnant. I sat in the washroom for half an hour trying to figure out what I was going to tell my parents and how life was going to be with a baby. Not only were they disappointed that I had left home, but now I had to tell them that I was going to be a mother.

I was just sitting there when I heard a knock at the door. It was Alex's little sister, Cassie, who was also a teen mom. In a loud voice she demanded to know whether I was pregnant or not. I slid the test under the door. A few seconds later I heard an exclamation of joy, followed by the question: "Can I tell my mom?" I sent her away so I could think. Still wondering how to tell my own mom, I heard the front door open followed by three sets of stomping feet. Cassie was bringing her mom, Raquel and a family friend, Melissa, and they started begging me to come out, so they could shower me with hugs. I reluctantly left the washroom with tears in my eyes. They were so caught up in their own happiness that they did not ask why I was crying.

Art by Natalie Helm

A few hours later I heard the phone ring. A familiar deep slurred voice came over the phone. "I will be home in a bit, baby," Alex said. I could hear that he had been drinking. Still shaken, I responded: "We are going to have a baby." But before I got it all out he hung up on me.

A week later I asked my mom to meet me for dinner. This was the most depressing and upsetting day of my life. I finally got it out. For the next five months, my parents pestered me to give up the baby – first abortion and then to adoption. My refusal killed them a little more each time. On my 17th birthday I called my mom to ask her to take me out. I heard, "Please do not call me anymore." Those six little words broke my heart. I felt like I had lost my family, and I looked at what I had replaced it with in disgust. I realized that I had left a clean house, plenty of food and love, for what?

For the next month I spent my time being hungry and wishing I was home. In early March, my mom finally called and invited me to go to Scotland on one condition: I was not allowed to tell my family I was pregnant. I agreed to go because it was my mom's dream. Two days later my mom took me shopping for my birthday to get clothes that fit. It was a good day but when I got back, Alex who was drunk already, yelled at me because I didn't get any extra money for food. Two weeks later my parents came to pick me up for our trip to Scotland. When I got in the car I watched as my mom's happy face suddenly turned sad at the sight of my black eye. I lied and told them I had fallen but I knew that my dad could see right through me. We left for Europe and my dad and I reconnected in some way, although he still wanted me to put my baby up for adoption.

After we returned from Scotland, I started spending the weekends at my parents' house. They were still disappointed with my decision, but happy that I was there and I was happy about it too. Two months later I was at my parents' place when I started getting a huge migraine. My mom read to me, trying to help me sleep. I don't remember much after that. But four days later I woke up in the hospital and I saw that I wasn't pregnant anymore. Then I blacked out again. Alex told me that I had a boy and I named him Nathaniel. He was a beautiful baby boy, four pounds nine ounces. All my friends came to see me. My dad didn't. He didn't want anything to do with my son. The next few days I spent getting better and seeing my son in the NICU.

When I was well enough to walk, my social worker and my mom took me to the foster home I was going to go to. I was miserable at the thought of living there. It wasn't a nice place – with a yappy dog and it smelled of bad cooking. I looked at my mom and told her I did not like it. She responded, "Jenny, you don't have time to be picky."

I went back to the hospital broken-hearted that I was not invited to come home. My mom called me that night and said: "Jenny, you are not well enough to take care of a baby. Tell your doctor you are coming home with me." I started to cry and I whispered, "Thank you so much." After I got off the phone, I ran to the NICU to tell my baby the good news. Even though he couldn't understand me, I could feel he was happy. The day after, my dad finally came to the hospital to pick me and my baby up to take us home. He said, "Jenny, only one week." I cried a little and replied, "Alright." After a week had passed, my dad came up to me and said I could stay for one more week. That night I asked him to hold Nate. Although he protested, I plunked the baby onto his lap. Ten minutes later, he told me with joy in his voice, "He looks like me." My dad put Nate to sleep and we had two nice days. When I was talking about leaving and started to pack, my dad came to me and told me to stop. He whispered with tears in his eyes, "Please do not leave. I lost you once and I will not lose you again."

Seven months later, I am still at home and happier each day. My life is getting better and my son is very happy. I am thankful I have my family. I am happy now and that is all I can ask for.

The Open Gate

Photo by Kayla Chaves

The open gate symbolizes a place where you are welcome to enter, to follow a path where you don't know what lies ahead. To me, that path represents life. As a mother, I don't know what's ahead in the life of my son. I can choose which way to go but I can't know if the path is going to be smooth or rocky, curved or straight. All I can really do is choose whether I will step through the gate.

Brooke Perkins

Tanner

To step into someone's life and help him raise a child at a very young age is an experience that changed my life. It is hard to explain the highs and lows, or the way I feel when this young boy looks up to me for advice, for help, for love and for companionship. I am happy to know what I have given up for him despite the struggles we've experienced together. It is a fact that even though we are not related by blood - we are all one, and we are a family.

I entered the house of my friend and met the man and his child who would soon turn my world upside down. I remember it just like it was yesterday. I was introduced to Kris and his four-year-old son, Tanner, one evening and I could not help but notice how the two of them looked so much alike, both of them troubled, small and skinny, with beautiful blue eyes. Both were quiet and very shy. Kris had a hard life raising his son alone for so many years. He had a hard time bringing discipline and structure into Tanner's life because he was so busy working all the time. That evening, Tanner and I sat side by side on the couch watching a movie, and all of a sudden he was not

shy anymore: he was laughing, I was tickling him, and we were having a good time. That was when I decided I was going to stay: Tanner and his father had chosen me, and I had chosen them.

Little did I know how fast I would have to grow up; I could not and would not be a bad role model for Tanner. He had experienced enough bad things in his life as his mom had disowned him, by choice, at a young age.

I soon realized that we could not live from Kris's salary and therefore I decided to to quit school. I started working full-time as a photo lab technician in Wal-mart. With this job came little time for friends or relatives. Kris was working mornings and I worked nights so we didn't have much time together. Tanner had not been attending Kindergarten until mid-year since his mom had decided not to enroll him, so I signed him up for school – better late than never. Money was still tight even though both of us were working, so we had no means of transportation. Every morning, for an entire year, I woke up and brought Tanner

to school on the back of my bike. Rain, snow or shine, he made it there everyday that year and into the start of the next year. Many times we did not have enough food to last us the two weeks between paydays, and often Kris and I would not eat to save food. I did not have much to offer at fifteen, but what I gave up for our family was everything I had.

That was not the worst of it. Tanner was in serious need of structure, discipline, and some major TLC (tender, loving care). He was constantly feeling unwanted. He tried to get attention the wrong way and lacked motivational skills to do well in life. Tanner was a very temperamental child and threw a lot of fits: intense, bad fits. Tanner was unsure how to handle new situations and Kris and I tried to enforce rules, bedtimes, and instill values that would encourage him to be a good boy.

To this day, Tanner has a hard time accepting rules and often has tantrums, but he is nothing like he was two years ago. Tanner and I have shared some bad times, but in the end, when he is upset, I look deep into those beautiful, blue eyes and just know he needs me, as I need him.

Raising a child, especially not your own, is a rollercoaster ride, with its up and downs, dangers and thrills; it just keeps on going once you have signed on. In my own life I have fought depression, and I still fight it to this day, sometimes wishing, praying, hoping to just be a kid again. But I know that if I had the choice, I would probably do it all over, but with the benefit of the skills I've gained throughout the years. This crazy lifestyle of mine keeps getting better and easier to hold on to; sometimes I wonder what life would have been like for Tanner if I hadn't have stepped in and shown him almost everything he knows. This ride is never going to stop because he is part of me now. He is in my every thought, every dream. He's in my future as well as my past; my memories are all about us as a family. This little seven-year-old, with his gleaming smile and amazingly funny personality, has broken down my wall, and now I think I'm the one who needs him to be part of my family.

Photo by Autumn Corona

Vinny Locsin

Life is Beautiful

Compassion for many is finding a way to relieve someone else's suffering. Often people donate money to the poor or give food to the homeless. But most of the time, compassion does not come out of a pocket; it comes from the soul.

I was born in Manila, the exotic central island of the Philippines. I make it sound enticing but it's really not the kind of place you would want to go for a clean, fresh breeze or crystal clear waters. But what you can find in the Philippines is a lot of love, a lot of spirit, and a lot of life.

In 1990, my family moved from Manila to Vancouver, and since then I have lived in one of the most peaceful and sought-after places in the entire world. But every Christmas, my family takes the stuffy, 15-hour flight to the Philippines to be with family and friends. The contrast between the two places is startling. Each year, I travel from a city where constant rain becomes a nuisance to a land where every breath of clean air is a blessing. In the Philippines, it's not uncommon to see people sleeping on the dirty streets, to witness disabled children trying to move without anyone's help, or to watch people die and be thrown into the sewers to rot. Life in the Philippines is not pretty, but, ironically, if you look close enough, you'll find that it is beautiful.

I'll always remember this one Christmas Eve in the Philippines. I was sitting in the car with my father at the wheel, my mother beside him; my sister and brother cramped in with me in the back. I was squished, nauseous and anxious to get home. A thunderous knocking rained onto the car. It was a crowd of beggars hoping to gain a couple of pesos.

Photo by Martha Clemente

You will not go a day in the Philippines without having masses of naked and dirty children knocking on your car windows to ask for some spare change. My dad scraped a couple of peso bills from his pocket and rolled down his window. He told them to gather around the car and then he said firmly, "Paghati-hatiin nong pera (share the money)."

When he reached out his palm, hands grabbed, voices screeched and bodies shoved. The beggars went after the money like wild hyenas fighting for a lone piece of meat.

Minutes later, in the comfort of clean clothes and a cushioned seat and in the comfort of an air-conditioned car, I asked my dad why things had to be this way. He simply replied, "Life is ugly." But as I was to learn, he had never been more wrong.

The next day, as we were coming home from our family's Christmas lunch, we saw the group of beggars from the night before. They were all standing together sharing what seemed like a few rolls of bread. And they were smiling and laughing with all the joy in the world. In each other's company, on that special Christmas day, everything made sense. In that moment, I knew I had just witnessed something beautiful.

My story isn't wild and suspenseful, nor is it lengthy or vivid. However, the message speaks volumes: Life is beautiful. In this life, we are blessed with the ability to care and to love. In this life, we are gifted with the spirit to show compassion, empathy, and kindness. In this life, we are rich with all the treasures of the heart and soul, we simply need to embrace it. Life should not be about turning away; it should be about looking beyond. There is beauty in all things if we are willing to see it.

Art by Gayle Oh

Witnessing & Observing

Mia Glanz
LACES

The bus pauses before the stop, then, with a smooth humming, it pulls alongside the solitary woman, outlined alone against a Main Street façade. She is all quilted coat and strawberry hair, impressive and ghastly. She represents the rain in her disarray with her loose lips and large body that the sun hasn't baked firm and supple. The crowded bus judges collectively, succinctly.

Please, I hope she doesn't smell.
What's in that huge bag?
Poor woman.

Vaguely she unzips her purse, fumbling the clasp with acrylic nails. She is leaning against the side as the bus pulls away, summoning composure, gripping the silver pole for safety. Lamenting, she addresses the driver in a distracted monologue.

"Oh, bus driver, I know I've got it in here somewhere. I've lots of change today. It's just that I have so much stuff in here it's really hard to get anything out of this bag. My daughter probably took it. She does that sometimes. Can you believe it, stealing from her mother? I'm so sorry, I always pay my fare. I really have it today, bus driver, I do. Oh, I'm so sorry, if you could hang on a sec."

"It's fine, lady. Don't worry about it."

"I just need to sit down. I know it's in here somewhere. I know I had some money in here, really. I always pay. Give me a minute."

She moves her heavy body in time to her words. She draws every eye on the bus as she sits, loud and frantic. The passengers are still and move quietly to accommodate her. But she is focused on her plushy stained bag, diving in and out with one stocky hand, pulling it open with the other. Bent neck, exposed and fleshy, unaware of her audience.

"Hold on, I have it here. Don't have to give me any charity. I always pay, it's true."

She disgorges the content of her purse, piling everything against the seat beside her. A few coins land on the floor and she bends over. She draws a deep breath, perhaps to prepare for another onslaught of words.

Quietly a man rises from his seat. He is slight and simply dressed, with a back smooth and straight, his gentle folds of pale skin only whisper of wrinkles. He takes poised steps and the bus burns silently with breath held in. An absolute silence as he moves toward the woman, free of pretension, full of soothing energy.

In a gesture poignant and strange, the small man reaches the woman and kneels before her swollen feet. He ties her undone laces, slowly and simply. At first she is distraught.

"What are you doing? No, you don't have to."

But gradually she falls silent and can only release a drained "Oh", a sound fat with melancholy. Together the bus breathes out with her as the man walks back to his seat and sits down.

Kai Ling Chieh

ON THE BUS

The bus is warm and stuffy, even though the windows have been forced open; the pressure of strangers' bodies is all around me. I'm hanging onto the slippery metal pole beside me as if it's a lifesaver, trying to avoid accidental physical contact with anyone in my meager five-centimetre-wide area of personal space. I check my watch for the time before I realize I don't have one. Looking around, I stealthily angle my head straining to read the upside-down analog face on the wrist of the bald-headed man sitting on the seat beside me. I make it a point not to talk to strangers.

The bus jerks to a stop and I am almost flung into the engulfing gaudy shawls of the woman next to me. I smile apologetically, though I realize that this might have come across as cheekiness as she turns away muttering something about teenagers and disrespect. I am distracted from her mumblings by the jostling group of teenage boys entering the bus and I inwardly groan. How is everyone supposed to fit into this over-packed vehicle? And how can teenagers be so amazingly irritating and obnoxious and loud? My questions go unanswered as the doors swing shut and the bus continues on its jerky route. The boys move further back chattering and laughing. At the next stop, a stooped old man in a cardigan enters the bus. His hair is soft white and his steps are unsteady and shuffling. He stands next to the boys, hands trembling on the pole in front of him. I feel sorry for him, having to stand while rowdy teenage boys are sprawled on the seats beside him.

"Here, sir, would you like my seat?"
I almost give myself whiplash craning my neck to see who has offered his seat to the old man. When I

realize that it is one of the boys who had managed to wangle a seat, I am even more astonished at the fact that the boy has spoken to a complete stranger than the fact that he has offered his seat. The teenager rises from the seat, mp3 player blaring so loud I can hear it over here. And the wrinkled brown face of the old man crinkles into a face-splitting grin as he thanks the boy profusely. This small, almost thoughtless act of kindness startles me. When I reflect on my previous thoughts I feel guilty and maybe even a little ashamed. What kind of world is this where people are scared of talking to other people on the street? How much does it hurt to ask someone on the bus what time it is?

When I next glance at the boy and the man, they have slid back into the same alienated detachment that exists between strangers on the bus, and for some reason this makes me inexplicably sad. As the bus reaches my stop and as I step down out of the bus and onto the sidewalk, I wonder if that tiniest moment of compassion will affect the teenager and the old man. I imagine the teenager walking away the same on the outside, but inside a better person. I believe that that moment of offering his seat on the bus would leave him with the understanding that he has done something right. This small action could be the catalyst for a series of reactions in the teenager. As for the old man, I imagine that he is safe with the understanding that there are people, namely youth, in this world who are compassionate and care for others. With this thought in mind, I promise to myself that the next time I see an elderly person on the bus, I'll step up, just like the teenager with the loud music, and give that person my seat.

Sophia Wong

David

With her baby in her right arm, the young son in front of her, and a large overstuffed tote bag hanging on her left shoulder, the young mother held up three fingers with her left hand.

"Take a seat anywhere you like," my mom said with a smile.

The woman smiled back and immediately threw down her bag on top of the nearest table. The loud thud sent the baby into tears, which in turn caused the other two patrons in the restaurant to turn their heads.

"Shit," the young mother cursed softly while her son calmly took the menu.

I watched the scene from the cash register. It was 3:30 p.m. on a hot August afternoon. My aunts and uncles, who also worked in the family-run restaurant, were already exhausted from the morning and lunch rushes. A construction site had recently opened up a few blocks from the restaurant, so every day at exactly 9:10 a.m. a stream of construction workers would come for their half-hour break, eat, leave and return at around 2:00 p.m. for their lunch hour. That, along with the usual patrons who came here nearly every day, added up to more than enough work for me, my mom, aunt and two uncles.

"Sophia! Stop staring at the wall and help your mom get some knives and forks!" scolded my aunt from behind me. "Be useful!"

"Sorry," I said. I grabbed three sets of knives and forks and went to the family's table.

"Okay, so two four-dollar breakfasts, both scrambled with sausage and white toast, three waters, one OJ, and an extra plate for the baby?"
The young mother nodded.

"Okay, she'll get the drinks," my mom said, pointing to me. I forced an awkward smile onto my face – the same smile I plastered on for all the customers since I had started working here at thirteen. I completed the drink orders and took a walk around the small restaurant to check on the other two guests. Both had already finished their meals and were enjoying their news-paper with their coffees. I drifted to the fridge where my mom was scooping red Jell-O into small dessert bowls.

"So…" I started, casually.

"So what," she snapped back.

"What do you want to say?"

"I don't know. I'm bored. I hate working here."

"Well, too bad. You're the only person who can help us because now you're not in school, you don't have a job and you're not lazy and stupid like Gordon."

I laughed. Gordon was my cousin and it was true: he was stupid and lazy.

It seemed as though he only left the house to buy food or video games.

"What are you laughing at?" mom said, "If you don't work hard in school, you'll turn out just as stupid as he is."

I rolled my eyes. Somehow she always found a way to ruin any good mood I was in. I glanced at the kitchen to see if any orders were ready, but none were. I then caught sight of a certificate that was taped to the wall beside the cash register. I wasn't able to read the small print, but the bold numbers read "1987", which was the year the restaurant opened.

"Wow, Mom. You've been doing this for twenty years now."

"Of course. How else are we going to make a living."

I shrugged. We'd had this conversation numerous times before, and I wasn't in the mood to start all over again. But I couldn't help but think of the younger version of my mom, the less knowledgeable and wise version, waiting tables for the same customers I have come to know since seventh grade.

"David, you're back again!" my aunt shouted from behind the register with a trace of amusement.

I turned my head to the entrance. David muttered and stuttered his usual inaudible words, staring straight ahead with his dark brown eyes and gray, bed-head hairstyle. His stained white and turquoise striped dress shirt was half tucked into his baggy beige trousers, and his socks in his open-toed sandals had tiny spots of gravel crusts. He walked to a table with four seats in the middle of the restaurant and pulled out a chair. Sitting sideways, he swayed back and forth, back and forth. The young mother and her son looked on, alarmed, but the other two patrons, both regulars and used to David's antics, didn't even look up.

"David," my mom said, calmly and quietly. He looked at her with his mouth open, still swaying.

"Please go to the back and take that table." She pointed to a table with two seats.

David stood up and walked over to the two-seater near the back. After a few seconds of more swaying, we made eye contact. He lifted up his hand to let me know he wanted something.

"Yes, David?" I asked as I walked towards him.

"C-c-coffee?" he asked.

"Okay," I replied. I got him the coffee (black and with no spoon, the way he liked it) and went back to my mom.

"Mom," I whispered, "why do you guys put up with him?"

"He's actually a good person, Sophia."

I was surprised by her answer. I wondered what she meant by "good person" because in my eyes, he was a moocher who rarely ever paid for his food – his sister did. David scared the customers and would always come in during those busy morning and lunch rush times and bug my uncle for food. Sometimes he would even come in

angry with his face flushed and on the verge of yelling (although I would never know why) and my mom had to put down whatever she was doing to calm him down. To put it simply, David was crazy, and yet my mom insisted that he was a "good person".

"What?" I said.

"I know he is crazy, but he won't hurt anybody. He gives me money when he has it. Sometimes he'll come up to me and say, 'Gail, how much do I owe you for the meal yesterday?'"

"Oh." I was dumbfounded. "I didn't know. I thought he just got away with mooching off you guys."

"Uh, no. He pays when he can. He is a good person. Crazy, but harmless."

"But doesn't he scare the customers too?"

"He does sometimes. But we are on the bad side of town. Most of the customers who come here aren't made of money, most of them are used to this."

She had a point.

"But Mom, this morning he came during the rush and wouldn't leave until uncle gave him a cigarette. Doesn't that annoy you?"

She laughed, "Of course! But we've known him for almost ten years now. Don't you think we're used to it? Besides, as long as his sister pays, there's no reason to kick him out. And you know he doesn't have a job."

"But you only keep tabs on his meals. You don't keep track of all the coffee he drinks." I did a quick calculation in my head. Assuming he got away with a free coffee a day, and this was an underestimate, that would make

around $150 lost each year in profit. Over ten years that made $1500.

"Oh, that's alright. One free coffee here and there won't hurt." She assured me. I went over my calculation again and scoffed.

"You know," my mom continued in a thoughtful voice, "not everybody is as lucky as we are. And he truly is a good person."

"I know, I know. You've said that a hundred times already."

"He is a good person," she repeated. Then she went back to scooping the remainder of the red Jell-O.

I stared at swaying David and his nearly empty coffee cup. This was somebody my mom believed to be a "good person." He picked up his cup with his dirty hand and tried to suck in the remaining coffee. When he was done, he carelessly set the cup onto the saucer and reached into his pocket. He took out a quarter, placed it on the table and started towards the door.

"G-Gail, I'll pay you when I can. Just rem-remind me."

"Okay, David. When's your sister coming?"

"Soon, I think."

"Okay then. You tell me when she's in town. Bye now."

"Okay," David said. He left. My mom looked at me as he walked out the door.

"See? He's a good person," she said, trying to convince me one last time. But the quarter on the table was enough evidence for me.

Aaron Leung

Baby Steps

That afternoon I noticed that the sun shone especially radiantly as its beams penetrated every shadow of the usually dark room. Its rays illuminated the floor with the power of a hundred stage lights bathing every corner in a sea of lights. But instead of spotlighting a violin prodigy or some breathtaking acrobatic stunt, today the sun shone brightly on a pair of feet – feet belonging to a 50-something year-old woman standing tall on the polished hardwood floor. To many, that does not sound like an impressive feat – I mean, it was one baby step in the grand scheme of things – but to the woman in mid-battle in her war against cancer, a former fully functional woman turned quadriplegic, it was a huge stride forward.

From her lips rolled the words of her favourite hymn and her smile radiated joyfulness and victory. Indeed, it was a victory, her refrain rising high above the valley of the shadow of death that had hung around in previous months. That day she was not the only one singing that tune. When she took her first step in months, family and friends surrounded her. Her brother and sister, for instance, were among those who had spent countless hours aiding her in everyday tasks such as bathing, feeding, sorting out medication and taking her to the doctor's office, among many things. There was her physiotherapist who prescribed daily muscle-strengthening exercises. Then there was her mother, a strong 85-year-old, giving emotional comfort and support to her daughter while at the same time battling her own emotions. These people had drastically changed their lives for the well-being of the one they loved.

When that first step rang on the hardwood floor, understanding hit me. I finally understood how powerful compassion truly is. Here was one woman diagnosed with breast cancer a long decade ago. She had her breast removed, and now was diagnosed with severe bone cancer, initially thought to be a mere muscle spasm in her neck. Here was a woman who was quadriplegic. And here was a multitude of friends and family visiting her every day, giving her emotional and physical support and prayers, and doctors and medical staff watching her condition and prescribing her medication and supplements to improve her health. Here was a patchwork of people working together to improve one person's life. And here she was on that day, her mouth stretched in a wide smile, her eyes bright, her laughter as charismatic as a child's, her once-paralyzed legs and feet standing firmly on the ground. Compassion is truly amazing.

Today, when I look at the photo of the scene, the sun still shines and the smile hasn't lost its radiance. Every time I peer at it I see hope ignited by the fire of compassion, torches held high by so many people, dots of light across this vast green and blue sphere so many call home. Yes, every time I see that photo, I see her smile, I see hope. The smile belonged to my aunt Julienne.

Dustin Osborne

My Aunt & Grandpa: a Ten-Year Journey

Ten years ago, my grandfather was diagnosed with mouth cancer. From that time his condition had improved a bit and then it had gotten worse, not just for him but for my aunt who was always there for him. My extended family and I have always gotten along nicely, and we still do. We take care of each other, and are always there for one another. When my grandpa was first diagnosed with cancer, the doctors gave him six months to live. Almost ten years later on December 6, 2007, at 3:30 p.m. he passed away. From the first diagnosis till Jack Osborne's death, the story unfolds as follows.

My aunt Wendy is the most loving, caring person in the world. She would do anything for anyone. Even if it did not benefit her in any way she would still try to help. Then came that fateful day of the diagnosis. My aunt knew it would be a huge task, but she loved her father, and would give anything to see him get better, and so they started on this ten-year journey together. During these ten years, my aunt provided incredible support for her father, Jack Osborne. She helped him in any possible way, including driving him to Vancouver multiple times a year to the cancer clinic to see him get better.

A little bit later in this journey, my grandpa was a so-called survivor of cancer. It was gone from his body. The surgeons had to operate on his jaw to remove all the cancer. He came back looking different because they had to take out part of his jaw. He went back to his good old, loving self again, and everyone was happy.

Yet again, in later years, he was diagnosed with cancer for a second time. This time it would not go away. My aunt and her husband Terry helped in any way they possibly could. They even gave him a part of their property to rebuild a house on. We had all put time into helping him rebuild and repair that house. My grandfather had just finished putting those last final additions when the cancer hit him severely. Therefore, they began again with several trips to and from Vancouver and back to the cancer clinic for more treatment. We all helped the best way we could, we all loved him a lot, and yet we all had to sit there and slowly watch him fade away.

My aunt was the bravest of us all. She had gone through hell and back to help her father; she had done everything possible. I remember one time when there was a leak in my grandpa's roof. My grandpa would have fixed it except he was stuck in a bed, not able to move or eat, and the leak was dripping on him. I was the only one able to go on the roof that day and stop the leak from landing on him. It was a very depressing day.

A few days later, I was getting ready for work and I had walk to the nearby school to wait so my mom could drive me to work. When my cell phone rang and it said "dad" on the call display, my heart sank. I answered the phone to my father crying and telling me to call in to work and say I wasn't going because my grandfather had just passed away. I broke down at that moment, but I didn't show it. The one thing I cared about the most was how my aunt was feeling because she went through everything with her father. In my opinion, she deserves an award of some kind for what she did to help my grandpa.

That day he died was a horrible day, it was a horrible month, and nothing was the same for a while. In time, things got better, but we all still miss him dearly, most likely my aunt more than anyone. So this is the story of my aunt and my grandpa and their ten-year-long journey.

Yisaiah Yuan
Same Old Lonely Season

The weather was unusual for Vancouver. A few of the trees in front of our porch were wielding their branches as if they were greeting the arrival of spring. The breeze was the kind that came from the mountain – cold but refreshing. I was lying in bed, reading *The Count of Monte Cristo*. Being so grateful for the beautiful day, my mom said she wanted to go out for a walk. Before she left the house, she asked me to eat an apple. I didn't want to eat anything at the time, but the apple was cut in half. And she took one half of it and left the other half. Was I forced to eat it? Well, I guess. No one wants to leave an apple to rot. While I was eating the apple, I adjusted the clock of our seldom used microwave to 1:20 p.m.

After one and a half hours, my mom still wasn't back. I felt a bit strange – what was so interesting that she would stay out for nearly two hours? Although I was wondering where she had gone, I did not think her disappearance was serious, or at least I thought she was not a child who might wander around the town and get lost.

It was nearly five o'clock and my mom was still not home. I began to worry although I told myself that there was no reason. She was a grown woman and had lived in Vancouver more than five years. But she was also a delicate and beautiful woman. What if she had encountered a criminal? What if she had felt dizzy and fainted just like it happened weeks ago? I phoned a few of her friends and they told me that she had not been to their places. I was desperate. I didn't know why I felt such trepidation. I was nervous. I could not imagine what might have happened to her. I had a thousand thoughts flashing through my mind. I thought of all those unpleasant things in this world – sickness, madness, violence. I thought that people are unthankful, disloyal, without natural affection, not open to any argument and puffed up with pride. I did not know why I thought about these things as if she had encountered one of them.

I put down the book. I was going to call 911. But then I changed my mind. What could the cops do? Instead I decided to go and find her myself. I wanted to discover the reason why I had such a strong and unknown feeling toward her. Isn't it awkward and shameful for a son to say that he cannot name this kind of feeling?

I put on a coat and grabbed the flashlight with the idea that I would spot her somewhere near Trout Lake chatting with someone. Or find her passed out in the vast field where no one had seen her or no one had cared to call an ambulance.

Wind blew hard at me. I could not move forward with my head up. When I had walked about 20 yards away from the house, I stopped. And I began to think how futile this search would be. I felt stupid.

I turned around and came home. Standing beside the door, I tried to think of what to do. But I didn't have a clear mind; I was just standing there numbly. Somehow I felt that it was my responsibility to make sure she was safe. If she was hurt, I would be the one to blame.

"I am out looking for you. Where have you gone? Sigh… makes me feel so worried."

I left the note just in case she came home without running into me so she wouldn't get worried too. I set out from the house towards Trout Lake. Two dogs growled at me through a fence as I passed by their territory. The guttural menacing sounds made me think of hitting them with stones. I was tempted but went on without stopping. On the streets, there was enough light that enabled me to see the path. But as soon as I entered the park, I had to turn on the flashlight and let its beam guide me. I went through a muddy field. The flashlight sweeping the dark, I looked for the colour red on the ground. She loves wearing red.

As I walked I realized the strength of the bond between us. Even though we hardly talk to one another, we view each other as a special person in our lives. I wouldn't have accepted that statement three years ago. Having not lived with her at the time, I was biased. And there had been a lot of misunderstandings between me, her, my dad and their parents. There are still many things we do not agree on. Like the way she washes the dishes. And I have told her many times to put the detergent in first before loading the washing machine with clothes. She always does the opposite.

Three years ago, when I landed in Canada, I talked to her like a friend. I would tell her about my feelings and share my opinions freely. But later, I discovered that she likes to twist things around to make herself look good, or to get favours. I felt betrayed that what I told her was not kept in a confidential manner. And when I unintentionally overheard her talking about me to her friends, she made comments that were untrue about her and me. Slowly I found that I could not trust her as the honest mother I had imagined her to be. I felt I was something she was showing off. And I shut her out. Our relationship remained cold and distant for about two years.

I kept walking and running. I was holding the flashlight in my bare hands and my fingers were frozen, as numb as my mind. A few people passed me but I didn't dare ask them if they had seen my mom. I didn't dare to shout out her name.

I didn't find her after circling around the lake and decided to go back home. I hadn't wanted to find her lying on the ground unconscious, but I could not ignore the fact that she was missing.

Everything was bleak. It might be best just to wait and hope.

I got home and saw that the lights were on. She was home. Seeing her all right was a huge relief alleviating all my distress. I was unusually emotional and she noticed that. She had seen my note. She was grateful and apologized for not giving me a call when she and her friend Alex went shopping at Granville Island. Alex is Caucasian. He looked a bit perplexed when I got home. I blamed him for not leaving his cell phone on. Later on, at the dinner table, my mom started talking to Alex about my story of searching for her. I know that the story will be told by her again and again. I know that the story will be twisted. I will let it be.

Photo by Shaylene Charleson

Blanket of Compassion

Art by Emily Lu

In my piece, the woman is holding a child close to her chest, to demonstrate the closeness to the heart in which one can hold another. Her arm is around the child in a protective manner, shielding him from the darkness. The black that surrounds them represents war and death and everything harmful in the world, while the glowing candle that she holds envelops them both – its glow protects them with warmth and comfort, much like a barrier that protects one from the dangers of the world.

Tiffany Chen

Beauty

Aflower in bloom is beautiful; its bright, stunning colours are attractive causing people to stop and admire it. However, as time goes by, the flower fades and it no longer has the eye-catching colour. Physical beauty is something that does not last – it is inner beauty that can last a lifetime. That is the lesson I learned.

I sat on the carpet in my room pondering what to write about in my essay. My stomach growled with hunger – it hadn't digested anything since eight o'clock in the morning. I had volunteered to do the 30-hour-famine, so I had been daydreaming about my favourite foods for almost the entire day. A mouth-watering aroma wafted into my room, causing me to abandon my homework and hurry downstairs, anxious to know what was for dinner. It felt like my birthday had come early: my mom had made samosas! The small, fried turnovers sat plump and juicy on a plate, waiting to be devoured. I squealed in delight like a little girl and gave the great chef a giant kiss on the cheek. My mom turned around and I noticed her tired eyes with dark bags underneath them. She smiled wearily and announced that she was going to take a nap. My smile faded as I watched her amble towards the living room sofa, her hair tousled, her clothes hanging on her tired frame, her steps slow and heavy. I peeked over the top of the sofa and saw that my exhausted mother had already fallen asleep. Sleep had taken over her body, and had transformed her tired, stressed face, turning it smooth and pale, almost making her look vulnerable, like a sleeping child.

When dinner time came, we all sat around our rectangular table chattering aimlessly. My mom scurried around asking everyone if they wanted seconds. With her apron on, and her face flushed pink, she looked full of life. My dad grinned and, looping his arm around my mom's shoulder, exclaimed "Don't you think your mother is beautiful?" Both of my younger sisters, Emily and Melody, laughed. I managed a weak smile. The image of my mother, tired and worn out, still lingered in my mind. How can she look even close to beautiful?

Before my mom was married, she was as bouncy as anyone can be. She worked in the mornings and studied in the evenings; she never seemed to tire. With her laughing eyes, freckled face, short black hair and boundless energy, everyone loved her. She was beautiful and my dad told me that he fell in love with her almost instantly.

When I was born, my mom hadn't changed much. Perhaps she looked a bit older and her energy had diminished a little, but she still smiled everyday and laughed a lot. However, when my two sisters were born, one after another, exhaustion started to seep through. It wasn't very obvious, but it was there.

Concerned, my dad did all he could to help take care of us, but that was difficult because he worked a full-time job. He tried persuading our mother to stop teaching at our church's Chinese school on Saturdays but she wouldn't listen. He argued that she needed more rest, but she wouldn't give up what she loved: teaching. With her charm and skill, she had won the hearts of her students. My amazing mom had been able to transform the students who never did their homework, help the students who were struggling with the Chinese language and guide the students who had talent but had never been able to show it. They all loved her despite the fact that she was tough, strict and gave lots of homework.

Every day, my mom would wake up early to prepare breakfast for my dad and then make our lunches. After she sent my sisters and me to school, she came back to walk the dog, do chores, run errands and take care of my grandma. When three o'clock came around, she rushed to pick us up. It did not just end there: after school, the three of us were engaged in different after-school activities. We all had swimming lessons and Chinese school, both of my sisters had school patrol, Melody had violin lessons, Emily and I had piano lessons. Day after day, our mom drove us to our different destinations. At home, she would watch us practise our instruments, making sure that we did what our teachers expected of us. She never once complained, but her body did. Strands of grey appeared in her jet black hair, a few lines creased her face and she needed to take naps between our lessons. Her boundless energy seemed to have reached its limit. She no longer looked her young, beautiful and energetic self. Time had taken a part of those things away.

Later that night, as I sat on the carpet finishing my essay, I heard laughter downstairs. Thinking that maybe we had visitors, I crept downstairs to get a better look. The kitchen was empty, but suddenly I caught sight of the source of the laughter. It was my mom, sitting on the steps of the porch with my dad, each of them holding a cup of steaming tea. The colours of the sunset cast a glow over everything – the image was stunning. The one thing that caught my eye, however, wasn't the beautiful sunset.

It was my mother's contagious smile, the insuppressible beauty that radiated from within, brightening the world around her – the kind of beauty that cannot be taken away by time.

Rachel Vale

Band Aid

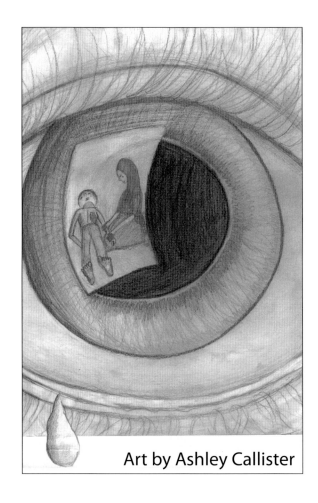

Art by Ashley Callister

The dictionary describes compassion as the expression of pity for another in trouble or distress. This definition applies to a moment in my life when I saw someone younger help an older person in need. I remember an incident I witnessed when I was in grade three, which may seem like a long time ago as I am now nearing the end of grade 10. But I remember it like it was yesterday. I was walking with a few friends down the driveway at my school. There was a small gravel patch on the hill before it flattened out into the parking lot.

As we were walking I turned to look to one side just as one of my teachers stumbled and slipped down the remainder of the gravel hill. She didn't show any signs of being badly hurt; there was just a small cut on her left knee with a trickle of blood. As we made our way over there, we saw my teacher attempt to get up. But as she tried to stand, she was slowly sinking back down. We found out later that she had fainted at the sight of blood. My mother, who is a nurse, quickly made her way to the teacher and told her not to try and stand but put her head between her legs and breathe deeply.

After several minutes the teacher seemed to be alright and the bleeding had stopped. But before she could get into her husband's truck, a shy little boy pushed his way through the crowd. He looked up at her with big brown eyes. Then he whispered to her not to worry, he had gotten hurt a million times. He then pulled a torn, wrapped Bandaid out of his pocket, unwrapped it gingerly and placed it neatly and gently on the teacher's wound. After that he put the wrapper back into his pocket, turned and walked away from the crowd without another word.

I know that this story isn't about a super-hero saving the world, but to me this is the greatest form of compassion where a younger child shows pity and love for another, even though that particular teacher was known to be tough and strict. In her time of need, the boy could look past their differences and show her kindness.

Kiera Schuller

Just Looking

It was an icy day in mid-December, the sky was dark and threatening and the cold air was too stubborn to give in to the warmth of the sun. I looked out of the window of a fancy black car, the streets looked back at me. Black pavement, dirty wooden posts and wet paper flying around in the wind. I sat in a car with Ali and her mother and we were driving to the downtown Eastside of Vancouver to drop off some boxes of clothing and supplies we had collected for a charity. The boxes were piled up in the trunk spilling over into the back seat and giving us no room to move or breathe.

As we turned a corner, I saw a person. It was an elderly man, dressed in a bright yellow jacket that was smothered in mud, jeans that had faded to a blank whitish colour and a hat that was ripped just above his left ear. His beard hadn't been shaved or cut in years and the grime on his face was thick. He was dragging a box, and from what I could see from my limited angle, the box held a pair of shoes that looked like they had once been white but were now a dull brown. The stripes on the sides were grimy but still a vibrant blue. The man walked on ignoring my curious stare as we drove by.

The car slowed in front of a church. Ali's mother found a parking spot and carried the boxes into the church. She left us in the car, but locked the doors to make us feel safer. I looked at Ali, raised my eyebrows and we both smiled. Sitting here in downtown Vancouver, we realized how lucky we were. I had the feeling that we had too much in our lives and that these people, who lived here without the same luck, had broken hearts. And we held the needle and the thread. We just didn't have the courage and willingness to mend their hearts because we were afraid of what it might pull us into. It seemed Ali and I didn't need to talk to one another. We both knew exactly what the other was thinking and we decided not to put it into words.

I looked out the window for a while and saw a man walking by. This was not the same man I had seen before. This man was young, and he had no beard. He wore a pale t-shirt that was a good size too small for him and, although it was about to rain, he held a vibrant green rain jacket in his arms. His cargo pants were too long for his short legs, the bottom part reached to the toe of his shoes, dragging on the muddy ground. The man, who seemed to be in his late twenties or early thirties, turned his face towards me. It took him a moment to realize that I was staring at him. At first glance his face showed a confused and dull expression. Not angry, but definitely not forgiving. But then he looked at the car and, seeing the boxes piled high in the back, his expression changed. I saw a glimmer of hope and he looked at me with a half-smile planted on his face. His eyes had a sudden softness in them and he nodded at me. At first I had been afraid of him, but then I saw the look in his eyes as he nodded. I will never forget that: the way this man tried to understand me, the way he accepted me, the way he was not angry that we were luckier than him. It seemed that he forgave me for having a better life. And that nod he gave me – a nod of respect, a nod of gratitude for the small part we played in helping him get back on his feet. I kept eye-contact with the man until the car pulled out of the parking lot and he began to walk away.

After we dropped off all the boxes, we drove into an alleyway to turn around and saw a woman digging through a heap of garbage. I looked at Ali and we just watched in awe. It was unbelievable that we lived in such a wealthy place with so many people who complained about not having toys or games or new shoes. And yet these people lived here as well. I could not see the woman's face. I just hoped that some of the things we had donated would go to her and that her luck would change.

Jordyn Senger & Melissa Morosse

Friends Again

It all started in grade seven after Melissa had just moved back to Princeton from Kelowna. She and Jordyn recognized each other right away since they had been childhood friends.

In the beginning the two friends were getting along pretty well but that quickly changed. Jordyn wanted to do something new with her hair. Since Melissa always had cool and crazy hairstyles, Jordyn was curious to know what would work with her hair and what kind of things Melissa could come up with. Unfortunately, the new hairstyle didn't work out that well. Yes, it was a stupid thing to argue about, but unfortunately it got worse. Melissa was offended when Jordyn changed her hair and it started to go downhill from there. Since Melissa was upset, she made the obvious teenage girl decision: she talked behind Jordyn's back trying to get her point across. To Melissa's dismay, Jordyn heard every word of it from the other friends and started fighting back, saying anything she knew would make the other upset. The situation escalated and was hard on all of their friends who were torn between the two. Jordyn and Melissa were trying hard to get everyone on their side. All this happened within the course of two days.

Jordyn and Melissa were both getting more and more upset with one another and by the second day, Jordyn didn't show up for class after lunch. Her teacher noticed that she was missing and went to find her. Together with the school counselor she found Jordyn in the bathroom, crying. Jordyn told them that she had been in a fight with Melissa and didn't want to go to class while she was so upset. The counselor took Jordyn to her office and asked her what happened. Then she found Melissa and talked to her separately. After she had heard both sides of the story, she tried to reason with the girls.

But they didn't listen.

They each believed that they were right. And they didn't want to hear the other's story. Then both of them started to cry. They didn't really want to stay mad at each other. They cared too much about their friendship and even though they didn't want to admit it at the time, they knew that they needed one another. So they confessed their true feelings and frustrations and eventually worked it all out together.

So, you're wondering: where does the act of compassion come in? Well, after the fight, Melissa wrote Jordyn a beautiful poem called *Build a Box of Friendship*. Jordyn kept it in a place where she wouldn't lose it and whenever she and Melissa were having trouble getting along, she took it out and read it. She kept the poem and actually put it to good use in a grade nine art class.

For one of the final art project, the students had to illustrate the lyrics of a song or a poem. Jordyn had no idea what to do until she remembered that special poem that had been given to her two years earlier.
So she built a box with plywood, painted it and dedicated it to Melissa for showing her what friendship, and of course compassion, really means.

That fight changed Jordyn and Melissa's perspectives on friendship and showed them that one single act of compassion can make a great difference in a person's life. That horrible, stupid fight was transformed into beautiful friendship that, they believe, will last for years to come.

Artwork by
Jordyn Senger

Melissa Morosse

Build a Box of Friendship

Into a box of friendship
To insure that it is strong
First a layer of respect
On the bottom does belong.

Then to the sides attach
In the corners where they meet
Several anchors full of trust
Devoid of all deceit.

The height of friendship can be measured
By the sides of four.
So make them all a longer cut
And the box will hold much more.

Now fill it up with courtesy,
Honour and esteem,
Understanding, sympathy,
And passion for a dream.

Add to that your honesty,
Emotions, joy and love,
And since they're so important
Place them up above.

But leave the box wide open
So all can see inside,
To learn what makes a friendship work
From the box you built with pride.

Just a Balloon

Art by Alisa Brandt

My image represents an act of kindness – stepping over the line, the boundary between the rich and the poor, to retrieve a balloon. It's just a balloon, but it's an act of kindness, and every little bit helps. The balloon, though seemingly worthless, means so much to the little girl. The tall businessman's side is the city, with his crisp clothes, green grass and tall buildings. The little girl's side is a rural village, perhaps even in a different country, with her dirty rags, mud houses, and thatched roofs. Taking the time from his busy schedule to help the little girl, the man carelessly lunges over the border, hand outstretched, and this is kind.

Marie Sekiguchi
What Are We Doing?

What are we doing?
Everyone has these days where
luck runs away from them:
pieces of crushed
confidence,
smashed faith and tears
align the kitchen table.

Here we are in this world.
*What are we doing? And **why**?*

Waves are washing shallow footprints away;
the glaring sunlight blinding hope;
the hourglass overflowing with sand.

She's dreaming; she's lost in her own dream;
doubt is a mist,
clouding her intentions;
she's scared.

And then there was him:
the relief of suffering felt,
his sweet criticism,
soft words exchanged;
he must be compassion.

She looks up at the crisp blue sky –
the sunlight no longer glaring at her,
she smiles.

What are you doing?

Art by Sarah Sun

Giving & Receiving

Rita

The Neverending Thread

A raindrop plunges
Into a pool of water.
Transparent, crystal-clear,
Welcomed by other droplets
In the pool.
Weaving magic, weaving communities.

A circle in the sand.
A circle drawn by us
Around our families, meaning to protect them
And care for them.
But if we took the time
To draw a larger circle,
We would let in many people
And care for the world.
The circle of love, life, arms encircling.

We are all brothers and sisters,
All related.
Learning to share, to banish selfishness.
Weaving the threads of love together.

Negative feelings diminish us.
Fraying ropes collapsing,
Breaking a whole braid.

Red, yellow, blue, green, orange, white.
All the colors of the flags.
All the countries in the world.
Tying us together
With love, peace, compassion.

Needle and Heart
Art by Carrie Cheung

Needle and Heart is an image displaying the power of compassion when others are in need. Darkness, a combination of black, jagged lines and ominous words, take up more than half the picture, symbolizing the immense and endless problems people may face. However, there is also help. The standing figure – who can be male or female, young or old, and any race – is using only a needle and his heart to create a shelter for those in need. The colourful quilt represents the good in the world – happiness, hope, peace and safety. The people within are benefiting from a person's selfless act of lending a hand, as well as taking part in creating a better world themselves – a world created with just a little needle and a lot of compassion.

Bennett Cheung

Ms. Peterson's Welcome

When my family first moved to Canada, it felt like we were moving into a world of unknown: we didn't have the slightest idea of what lay in store for us. We had no friends, nor any family to guide us through this transition period. The biggest changes we felt when we arrived were not due to the differences in language but in lifestyle. The home that we had bought was located in a suburban neighbourhood surrounded by tall oak trees and other one-storey houses. Back in Hong Kong, my family had lived on the 20th floor of a 40-storey apartment building. However, as soon as we settled in, we were greeted by a friendly middle-aged woman who went by the name of Ms. Peterson. She immediately made us feel welcome in this strange new society.

Ms. Peterson always wore a smile on her face, bringing happiness to all those around her. She often spent her time tending and watering her vibrant flower garden. There were all kinds of flowers that bloomed through every season, providing a never-ending cheerful atmosphere that suffused the whole neighbourhood. On each Christmas Day, I would find a small gift-wrapped box left inside our mailbox. Upon opening the present, I would come across a small stuffed animal resting beside a budding flower bulb, and a card wishing me and my family "Merry Christmas". On other occasions, Ms. Peterson invited us into her home for cookies and a cup of tea. During those times, she would share with us some very entertaining stories. She would tell us of the misadventures of her cat, or of her childhood with her brother. Her stories always made me laugh and I had the best of times.

One day in November when the leaves began to wither, we noticed a slight change at Ms. Peterson's household. The flower garden looked neglected; the colour of the flowers seemed to fade. We noticed many different cars stopping on her driveway, but Ms. Peterson's house stayed silent. Once we met Ms. Peterson's brother and asked him what was going on. We learned the grave news that Ms. Peterson was suffering from chronic cancer, and was currently bedridden. He informed us that her condition was severe and she was unlikely to regain her health and active lifestyle. He also told us that he was organizing a millennium party for her because this had been one of her dreams. We offered to pitch in.

My family felt that it was time to start giving back some of the love and affection we had received. Ms. Peterson had welcomed us with open arms at a time when we most needed friends. Now, she was facing a dark time and needed help. My mom had heard of a herbal medicine called Saussurea laniceps, or snow lotus, that was thought to strengthen one's inner defenses against cancer. We became part of Ms. Peterson's support circle just as she had been part of ours. We kept her company on weekends, we brought her herbal supplements, food and encouragement. Often, Ms. Peterson's nephews and nieces were visiting; the driveway was always in use. It didn't surprise us that Ms. Peterson had many friends and family members who loved her. Her attitude made her an incredibly loveable person. Compassion was truly present in that circle and we were fortunate to be a part of it.

At the turn of the new millennium, we attended Ms. Peterson's party. Although she was weak, she was at the peak of excitement and she told us that there were no words strong enough to express how fortunate and thankful she was – the party was everything she had dreamed of. Ms. Peterson stayed strong for another five months, before she lost her battle with cancer. Though she has moved on, we will never forget Ms. Peterson who was our beacon of light guiding us to a new place where we could belong.

Lucy Wang

Ting's Generosity

No matter whether one is old or young, rich or poor, one's kindness from the bottom of the heart is a miracle. Some acts of kindness may seem trivial, but they are felt deeply by the people they touch. Since my visit to China, I have been truly inspired by my compassionate cousin Ting.

Between the two of us, Ting has always been more mature, decisive and responsible although she is younger than I. She also loves to help others. Since she was twelve, Ting has had the responsibility of taking care of her baby sister when her parents were busy working. In truth, I was aware of the fact that Ting's family had been having economic difficulties. Yet never did I imagine that the condition was so dire.

Last summer, during my visit to China, I was shocked to discover that she had dropped out of school in an attempt to help with family errands and support her sister's education. I found that Ting, in addition to babysitting her sister, was selling ice-cream at a street stand, bearing the brunt of the over 28-degree temperature. When I first saw her, I barely recognized her. Days of standing in the scorching sun with gusts of wind that kicked up sand that felt like daggers slashing one's face, had left her face discoloured and her skin fragile, peeling and dry. I tried to help Ting by selling ice-cream with her, but I got sunburned in one single afternoon: her old beach umbrella could not shield us. In addition, the sales were utterly disappointing. For the entire afternoon, Ting only sold two ice-cream sticks, with only 20 cents profit. However, regardless of how hot and thirsty she was, Ting was unwilling to lose any money by enjoying an ice-cream stick herself. She explained that she wanted to save money to buy a new beach umbrella, a new pair of sandals (her old sandals were held together with stitches of thread), a new hat for her sister and some new stationery since her sister was going to school in the fall. Since Ting didn't want history to repeat itself, she vowed that she would try to keep her sister in school. From the longing look in her eyes, I couldn't help but wish that her dreams would come true. I was touched by the fact that even under such adversity, Ting was able to stay optimistic and work persistently towards her goals by saving every penny she earned. Unfortunately, Ting's simple goals all had to wait after one unexpected incident.

That summer, the sudden sickness of an old lady in the neighbourhood shocked the whole village. The lady was diagnosed with an infection that expanded from her fingers all the way to her kidneys and she need to have a treatment to flush her kidneys to stop the further development of the infection. But such a process required a lot of money, an amount that no family in the village could afford. Learning of the tragedy, all the relatives, friends and villagers donated money to help.

What surprised me was that upon hearing the news of the old lady's sickness, Ting, without hesitation, donated all of her savings of 70 dollars. Befuddled, I asked her, "What about your beach umbrella and your sandals? What about your sister?" Ting replied, "My needs can wait, but the sickness of the old lady can't. If her treatment is delayed, she may die. As for the things I want, my umbrella and sandals can last for another year. If they break, I can stitch them up. And for my sister's school supplies, I will find another job in the fall."

I was and still am deeply moved by Ting's situation and her acts of compassion. Even with her own economic problems, Ting was unwavering in her decision to donate all her savings. Although seventy dollars may seem like an insignificant amount, they represented Ting's caring heart. Having witnessed her unselfishness, I am inspired to give back to the community. This experience has changed my perspective on what I want to be in the future. Now I want to become someone who can help others. Every day, I'm working hard toward my goals and at the same time, I am praying for Ting, hoping that she can fulfill her dreams.

Nikita Morgan
Three Pieces of Cake

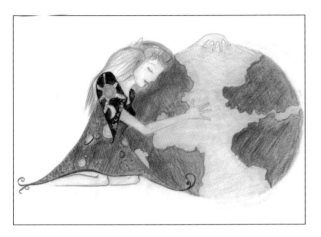

Art by Sierra Massey-Nesbitt

Every Wednesday, my mom and my aunt Shelia go to AA meetings. On my aunt's fifth anniversary of being sober, I decided to go with them. Together with other family members, we all went to the meeting to show and tell my aunt how proud we are of her. It was an emotional affair. Her children said things that really touched her and made her and many other people at the meeting cry. After everyone talked about their past, we gave Aunty Shelia a cake we had brought for her. She helped to cut it, and my cousins and I handed out the pieces.

There was still a lot of cake left after everyone had eaten and I told my mom that I was going to take the leftovers home. She asked me if I was really planning to eat them and I replied that I would save them for later that evening. I wrapped the plate in foil and we made our way to the bus stop. It was very cold outside; it was almost the end of November. After we boarded the bus I got tired of holding the cake and told my mother about it. She said to me, "I knew that would happen. Why don't you give the cake to someone who wants it?" This seemed like a good idea and I planned to give the cake away at our bus stop.

When we got off the bus I looked around and saw three homeless women. They were sitting on the steps in an entrance to a shop, huddling close together under a blanket to keep warm. I noticed that they were homeless and cold, but they also looked happy to be together. I walked toward them with my plate. I had three pieces of cake and thought that the three women would be perfect recipients. They accepted my offering with huge smiles. Then the woman sitting on the left told me that it was her friend's birthday. She pointed to the woman sitting in the middle and said to her, "See, I told you that you would get a cake on your birthday." My mom and I said, "Happy birthday!" and then turned to go home. We were almost in tears walking away from the women who were chatting happily and eating the birthday cake.

March against Homelessness   Photos by Lina Martin-Chan

Bella Molineux

Vinnie's Story

On a Monday in April, a man named Vincent Turner walked into my father's comedy class. My dad had been teaching comedy for over five years in downtown Vancouver, but had never come across anyone like Vincent. Vincent walked in mid-class and explained his situation: "I have uh, ten dollars in my pocket, I'll give that to you right now and then uh, I'll bring more next class and pay it off for you."

The six-week class costs $300 but my dad didn't care. He could tell just by looking at Vincent that he was an interesting character. He wore dirty, worn-out army pants, had shoulder-length messy hair, and had sores all around his unshaven mouth. And when my dad glanced out the window, he saw an old bike leaning against the wall, with stuff attached all around it. There was bag after bag filled with everything you could think of: clothes (especially shoes and hats), bags of food, little knick-knacks, everything. My dad simply could not resist taking a look at what this man had to offer in the field of comedy.

By the third week it was obvious that Vincent was homeless. But what amazed my dad (and not to mention everybody else in the class) was that this didn't get him down. He seemed to be happy no matter what. He always showed up to class with a smile on his face and a little bit of money in his pocket. During the fifth month my dad and Vincent knew each other, Vincent called my dad at home and told him that he had been beaten and was doing very poorly living on the street. Coincidentally, the next day was my father's birthday, so he invited him to come to Bowen Island for the night, meet the family and mingle with some friends. So that's what happened. Vincent came and met my brother and sister and me, along with many family friends. The next day it became official: he was moving in.

Moving Vincent into our house was hard. You wouldn't imagine that. He was homeless, so how much stuff could he have? But his bike was really heavy and it was my dad's job to take it from downtown Vancouver to Bowen Island. Vincent left it for him at the acting centre where my dad worked. So he had to ride the bike about six blocks to the bus stop and then take it to the ferry. After that he had to walk it to our house which was only a short trail away. Once my dad got the bike to our home, Vincent packed his things into his new room. His room was on the bottom floor. It had been my brother's room, but he was barely ever home. So it was ideal for Vincent to have it.

After only three days it was like he had always been part of the family. We even gave him a nickname: Vinnie. But our family explained to Vincent that he had to change his ways in order to get something out of living with us. For one, he had to quit doing drugs. It was obvious from the sores on his mouth that he did cocaine, and maybe other drugs. And we were determined to help him kick the habit. To help him take his mind off drugs, we set out to find him a job. My dad worked part time in construction with a good friend named Jim. So my dad asked if Vinnie could work with him, and Jim agreed.

Working hard labour from 8 a.m. to 3 p.m. was hard for Vincent especially during the time he was trying to quit drugs. But it definitely helped. He was off drugs in two weeks, switching over to pompom cigars. Working also gave Vinnie some income. He used most of his money to help us pay the rent and buy groceries. He was definitely a big help around the house and a joy to live with.

Vinnie bonded with everybody in the family. He and my dad spent many hours together working, and of course my dad still taught him comedy on Mondays. My dad also lent Vincent shirts when we were going out, and Vincent wanted to make somewhat of an impression on people. He and my mom also bonded. When my dad would go away to work as a comedian, Vinnie would often use the opportunity to play my dad's guitar for us. He wasn't the best guitar player. In fact he was somewhat dreadful. He was banging on the guitar strings and singing out of key but my mother and I still enjoyed it because of Vinnie's upbeat, happy personality. We couldn't help noticing how he glowed when he picked up the guitar and attempted to play music. When it came to my brother Zac, he thought that Vincent was really funny and fun to be around. My sister Nichole was a bit sketchy with him at first, but easily warmed up to Vinnie's kind heart and good intentions. My relationship with him was something else altogether. I loved having Vinnie around. He was always there for me to play games with. My friends liked him, and he always gave me a good laugh. We spent lots of time together and went for walks almost every day.

Vinnie was very grateful that we were taking care of him and he never hesitated to say thank you. He said thank you almost every day when he was eating a home-cooked meal made by mom. He was very happy. Months that felt like days went by and it wasn't until Christmas day that I realized how much he cared about us.

Christmas Eve is the one day of the year when the whole family gets together and has a nice dinner at the table. We had never celebrated this holiday with anybody from outside our family before but, by then, Vinnie was family. We played crib, ate fondue, and laughed together until we went to sleep. In our family at Christmas, it is a tradition that we three kids go down in the morning and check out what everybody got before waking up our parents. When my sister and I woke up my brother, we saw something we hadn't expected under the tree: Presents stacked up to two feet high all around. But everything on top was wrapped in newspaper. It was obvious that they were all from Vinnie. But we were shocked at how many presents there were and the obvious effort that was put into it all. When he woke up and we thanked him, he was really modest and just blushed at how thankful we were. Although this was years ago, my family still has some of the presents Vincent gave us. I still have the book *Wringer* by Jerry Spinelli, his favourite book. My mom treasures the picture he made for her and my dad has kept his gift: a pair of old shoes. Each present showed the connection we had with him and that made them all the more special.

Another month went by and we got in touch with Vincent's parents from Ontario who hadn't seen or heard from him in two whole years. They helped us pay for a flight and in mid-February Vinnie left. It was a really sad day for all of us. Lots of tears, but we were all proud at what we had done. Vincent left our house a different person. He now had better clothes, his hair wasn't as messy, and he no longer had sores around his mouth. He left with better quality things from Christmas Day and had less to carry, believe it or not. But what didn't change at all was his outlook on life. His happiness and good spirit. And the great quality he had: no matter what happened to him, he always thought of the good things.

It was no wonder his favourite song was *Tomorrow* from the *Annie* soundtrack. He always had it in his head that things would get better tomorrow. I think our whole family was left with that basic message.

Ellen Kim

Giving Means Everything

One summer, when my family visited Korea, we decided to explore a historic site—an ancient Korean village preserved since the old dynasties. It was one of the hottest days of the year and the place was located on a mountain. On that day I experienced the worst heat imaginable. And I also witnessed an act of kindness that has had a very powerful impact on me.

After five grueling hours of walking up and down the historic site, my family finally decided to go home. My mom, my sister and I were all exhausted and we were in a hurry to go back to the comfort of our car. However, my dad had other plans. He singled me out to go and see one last historic building with him. Now, I like learning about history and all, but walking around in the boiling sun for five straight hours with melting flip flops wasn't really keeping me happy. I was also walking with a limp since blisters had appeared on my foot throughout the day.

By the time my dad finally finished telling me about the history of the last building, I was not in a pleasant mood. I went ahead of him as we walked along the road leading to the parking lot. While I was angrily stomping down the mountain, I passed by a mentally disabled homeless man, scrunched up against the sidewalk. He had a numb smile on his face, and he made unusual grunting noises as his bent arms swung back and forth, back and forth. He scared me, so I avoided getting too close to him. As soon as I passed him, he was off my mind.

As I continued on my way, my guilty conscience got the better of me and I looked back to wait for my dad. He was coming down, and he was approaching the homeless man. I called to him in impatience, "Dad, hurry up!" And my dad started to jog. He passed by the homeless man, but he stopped after a couple of steps. He reached into his pocket and took out some bills. He took a few of them, put the rest back in his pocket, and ran up to the man. He dropped the bills into the yellow basket in front of the man, which had only held a couple of coins. Then he ran down and caught up with me. I looked at my dad with a sense of awe. I'd never thought that my dad would do something like that. As I kept staring at him, he sighed to himself and pulled out the rest of his bills. He handed all of them to me and told me to go give them to the homeless man. I was a little nervous to go so close to the disabled man, but my dad encouraged me to go back. I didn't want give the impression that I didn't want to give the money, so I ran back up.

As I dropped the bills hurriedly into the yellow basket, I looked into the homeless man's eyes. I thought that he'd be looking at me, but instead, he was still smiling into the emptiness, his face turned away from me. At that moment, an immense wave of sympathy washed over me. His disconnection from the world around him was my sadness for that second. I realized that it wasn't the man's fault for being in the state that he was, and that I had no reason to fear him. Instead, I had every reason to feel sympathy for him and help him.

Other than gaining a new-found respect for my dad, I learned one big thing from those few minutes. I learned about the joy it brings to help someone. Even though I was cranky that day, helping that homeless man in a small way brought me a sense of contentment. So during the rest of the walk down the mountain, I couldn't help smiling to myself.

From that day on, I have conducted random acts of kindness to strangers. Although it's not frequent, every time I do it, I never fail to feel fulfillment in my heart.

Eunice Wong

Book Fair

I remember a time when there was a book fair at our school library that went on for a week. In the mornings of that week, each class would make its way, in order by division, in single file to view and make a list of all the books the students wanted, so that we could go home to our parents and beg them to get us books. Once I went back home with a paper explaining that a CD I wanted was only seventeen dollars. I made my case about how cheap it was but my parents didn't buy it for me. Of course, they figured its title *Children's Saturday Tunes* was enough evidence of its value. After that time I knew only to ask for books, and only educational books at that. However, as my posse would walk through the aisles, we would linger around the do-it-yourself book section. Together we would pore admiringly over pictures of all the things we could make. These pictures never made it back to any of our homes. So I always wondered why the librarian stocked up on craft books every year. I don't think that anyone ever bought any. Our parents believed that fourteen pages of crafts cannot hold a girl's interest very long. Hence I stuck with my very safe – and cheap – re-readable *Franklin's Adventures* books.

When I was taking a break from my friends and their thrills, I would sit quietly in the library and read storybooks. Most of the others played outside, but there was one person who appreciated the books as much as I did. Gary was my friend's brother who often sat and marveled at the Japanese Anime books. He was a talented artist who loved to immerge himself into the world of Manga. Every year he would lust after a book. It was the same kind of book, but every year it seemed to get a little bit better. This book cost a whopping fifty dollars, more than his mother would ever afford, much less spend. But I could tell that he wanted that book, he wanted it more than any of the books my friends and I lusted after. Gary was very independent. The other boys in his class looked up to him, to his strength and ability to stand up for himself, especially with the teachers. Unsurprisingly,

the teachers did not appreciate his defiance quite as much. My friends did not like Gary, but I didn't mind his company in the library. He lived with his sister and their mother in a small house with overgrown plants. From what his sister had told me I knew that their mother didn't have a very good sense about spending money. It wasn't that she had too much to spend. But useless trinkets and cups and delicate things were plentiful while daily supplies were scarce. Gary and his sister did not often receive gifts. When they did, the gifts came from their father who only visited them rarely.

On the last day of the week during the book fair, an open house was held at the school and the books could finally be shown to the parents. Everybody came. Most of us dressed up for the occasion, ready to flaunt our special after-school clothes. That year I was unusually determined to break the rule that kept my parents from purchasing "cool" books. We could learn how to make bracelets from a single page in less than an hour, could we not?

In the end, I lost the battle. My plastic Scholastic bag contained one *Math Helpers* workbook and one *Junie B. Jones* novel. But someone else got what he wanted. My dad had bought the Anime book for Gary. I was very surprised. They had met only a few times when my dad had given him and his sister a ride home. I felt cheated. Gary was not even his flesh and blood, but I was. And my dad had only seen Gary sitting and looking at the book and heard him asking his mother. I had described the book I wanted in detail and had presented my case to him repeatedly over the week. I was furiously jealous and began to believe that my dad liked Gary better than me. But then my dad quietly explained. He said that sometimes you have to do something for someone else. It just felt right. And I wasn't jealous anymore. I looked at my dad and I felt glad.

Lara Wong

Cinderella's Glass Slipper

When Jenny hugged me with tears of joy in her eyes, thanking me for my generosity, I wanted to drown myself in a sea of misery and guilt. My selfishness and vanity had been mistaken for an act of compassion. Although at the time, the shame was overwhelming, I know that this experience has contributed greatly to making me a more compassionate person.

Every Saturday, Jenny, a new young Filipino immigrant came to our house to help with the cleaning. Like many other Filipino immigrants, she was a nanny and worked for another family during the rest of the week. When she first came to our place, a friendship was formed and when Jenny came on Saturdays it was as if she was part of our family. We soon learned of the many struggles she faced living in Canada with a very low status. The family she lived with didn't treat her with respect and as a foreigner with a domestic worker visa, she wasn't paid a large amount of money. Yet she always arrived at our house with a big smile and sang pop tunes while cleaning the bathroom. Although she didn't have very much she was very generous and sometimes shared her delicious Filipino lunch with me. She never complained but often sought out my mother when she needed someone to talk to.

I have always had more possessions that I needed. And when I wanted something else, I always got it. Growing up in the Westside of Vancouver, this life style was the norm for most of my classmates. Every season all the girls would have a new wardrobe, and many had hot tubs and trampolines in their backyards.

One day I needed a new pair of runners and my mom took me to the store. Since I had a hard time deciding, my mother ended up choosing for me – a blue-grey pair of runners with a metallic mesh covering. I thought they

looked pretty cool and wore them to school the next day. My classmates noticed at once but some of them said the shoes looked funny. Looking down on them I became aware that the metallic blue mesh looked like the eyes of a fly: big and bulging fly eyes. I would not wear those runners again. We could not return them and when my mom got upset with me, I accused her of forcing me to buy them and threw them at the wall. I got a new expensive pair of runners and the fly-eye shoes disappeared into the closet.

As the weeks passed, I started to notice that Jenny was losing weight and her joyful spirit was beginning to wear out like the ragged runners she wore. Something was weighing down the corners of her mouth when she tried to smile. My mom sat her down over tea and cookies. It turned out that her live-in family had not been paying her and there wasn't anything she could do since she had nowhere else to live. At the same time, her grandfather was sick in the Philippines and her family was expecting Jenny to be making enough money to cover some of her grandfather's medical expenses. There was hardly enough money for Jenny to feed herself and everything she owned started to wear out and needed to be replaced. Her jeans were ripped at the seat and the Sun Run t-shirt I had given her for housework was faded from too many washes.

At the door lay her runners, permanently grey and brown from trudging in the rain and mud, the shoe laces chewed away. A gap at the point of each foot exposed her big toes and allowed water to seep in. My mom could not let her go home like this. She searched through the closet for an old pair of shoes and came across the ugly fly-eye shoes. Quickly, my mom waved me over. "Do you think these will fit Jenny?" she whispered. I was just about to say, "You are giving them away? What if I need them?" Suddenly I caught sight of the shoes by the door and I nodded. I knew the runners would fit Jenny perfectly. Her feet could not be bigger them my size five. When Jenny joined us downstairs after her work was finished, my mom casually handed her the shoes. Not wanting to embarrass Jenny or me, my mom said, "Lara grew out of these before she could even wear them. Do you want to try them on?"

A glimmer of light sparked in Jenny's eyes and even before reaching for the shoes she ran to hug mom. When she pulled away there were tears running down her cheeks. She held the shoes in her hand as if they were the most beautiful things she had ever seen. Crouching down to put them on, she sobbed, "I was praying for my shoes to last the rest of the winter because there is no way I could afford new ones." Wiping off her tears, she stood up. The shoes fit perfectly, like Cinderella's glass slipper. Jenny's face was glowing, and the shoes looked beautiful then, even to me.

"Are you sure you don't need them?" she asked. I could not look at her anymore. The same shoes I had thrown at the wall and vowed never to wear had brought such happiness to Jenny. She was grateful for them, grateful to me and my mom, but I had done nothing. Absolutely nothing except for being ungrateful.

It took me a while to notice but this experience has taught me how to be more compassionate. I used to think that compassion was only about sponsoring children and feeding the poor. I had overlooked the small things because I had never thought they could mean so much to anyone. Now, whenever I find myself complaining about something I have or don't have, I always remember the tears that streamed down Jenny's face and the way she danced out of my door that day.

Photo by Becci Delacruz

Photo by Raymond Wu

Lauren Siegel

Thirteen

I awoke on my thirteenth birthday to a brisk March morning. Becoming a teenager seemed such a big deal to everyone. It is made out to be such an important milestone towards becoming an adult, but I didn't feel any different.

I have always looked for opportunities to spend some time with my mom, just the two of us. As a special treat on this day we decided to go to Granville Street and buy pastries at a fancy bakery. I had twenty dollars of birthday money to spend in any way I chose. I watched the city change from gold to grey out of the window of the car. As large houses with vast lawns faded from view, I caught glimpses of street people, alone and without hope. I wondered how some people could have so many things and others so little. Could these homeless people live a happy life without the riches other people had? These thoughts drifted through my mind and vanished as we pulled up to the bakery window stocked with treats.

I followed my mom into the bakery, breathing in the sensational smell. I scanned the counter full of pastries covered in pink icing. It was such an enchanting place, such a luxury. My thoughts returned to the homeless people and I wondered if they could ever experience this feeling. We bought some pastries and started to walk back to the car when I noticed a homeless man sit-ting on the sidewalk. He was quite young, I guessed him to be about twenty-five years old. He had a cardboard sign with roughly printed letters saying that he had AIDS and was asking for spare change.

I felt a sudden urge to give him the remaining five dollars of my birthday money and asked my mom to take the money out of her purse. She asked me what I wanted to buy, and I told her about my idea. She asked if I was sure that this was what I wanted to do and I insisted that this was my wish. My mom watched as I handed the young man the money. She saw a genuine smile spread on his face, and on mine. She understood that I was deeply moved by the desire to bring relief to this distressed person.

We all need to allow these feelings and impulses to help others flourish. I think we often suppress them, not wanting to be bothered or embarrassed. We get into the habit of ignoring our ethical sense. It would take an effort to change our habit of not acting, but if we could, imagine how different the world would be! We must remember that those who are less fortunate are still human beings who deserve our consideration and respect.

Perhaps there is still hope for a new generation: we could do things differently and our society would become more caring.

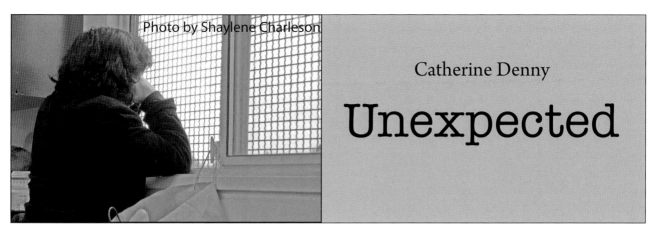
Photo by Shaylene Charleson

Catherine Denny

Unexpected

I remember it as an early, bright morning in August, with the sun highlighting the dark silhouettes of tall buildings and the traffic pulsing rhythmically. I was in the front passenger seat of the family car, regularly turning up the air conditioning while trying to concentrate on my book. My mother was in the driver's seat and rummaged in her purse for sunglasses while waiting at a stoplight. The light flashed green and she slid the glasses on her face before deciding that we needed gas and turning into a station down the street. The car pulled up beside the pump and I continued reading while she got out to fill up the gas tank.

As I sat in the car, my mother went into the gas station's store where she was to experience the sort of rare kindness and compassion that does not seem usual. She went to the counter to pay for the gas purchase and handed the clerk her cash card expecting it to be returned momentarily and that she would be on her way. But because of a technical error, the machine did not recognize the card and that did not happen. After repeated unsuccessful attempts, my mother promised to withdraw cash from the bank and return, offering to leave her wallet with the clerk as a sign of reassurance. The clerk declined that offer and said that this was unnecessary, that she felt she could trust my mother who turned to leave with every intention of coming back to deliver the money.

But before she made it to the door, the woman behind her in line did something so remarkable it is worthy of mention, again and again. Without hesitation, she insisted that she pay the full amount that was owed for the gas.

Now, this woman did not appear like she really would care that much about others, or that she would regularly assist them when they needed it. She was young and provocatively dressed, in a short skirt and high boots and had heavy make-up, as if she could be some sort of call girl or escort returning after a night of work. My mother thanked her for the gesture and assured her that she was able to pay, but found the woman's position was unshakable. "Please, I see that you have a child waiting in the car, let me pay for you." My mother finally accepted, and I still remember the expression or sheer disbelief and awe on her face when she told me about it. And I experience the same emotions each time I recall what happened, because I now realize that compassion can be found in the most unexpected places.

But what determines if compassion can be expected from someone or not? We use one's appearance as the main tool for judging, though logically, appearances have no effect on compassion at all. How do we arrive at the conclusion that what is inside translates correctly to the outside? How one looks does not hinder or increase someone's ability to be compassionate. But is it so horrible that we think that way?

By calling these acts unexpected, in a way they become even more powerful. We notice them more and take time to consider them. They surprise us when they happen. And if that's what it takes for them to have an impact, then it's unfortunate we aren't surprised every day.

Manjima Salim

A Drop of Compassion

Through the course of our lives, most of us go along alone, in our own world. But every now and then something happens, an interaction that connects lives, maybe only for a minute. It is a great experience – it illustrates the power of compassion.

Many years ago, when my father was a day away from graduating from university and everyone was busy with the excitement of leaving behind the years of strenuous studies, something tragic happened. His friend's cousin fell ill and was in desperate need of a blood transfusion.

However, in the anticipation of the celebrations to come that night and in the process of getting ready for the graduation day, no one was able or willing to donate blood. My father was a strong-hearted man and saw how anxious his friend was, so he traveled with a few others to the specialized hospital a few hours away to help the friend in need.

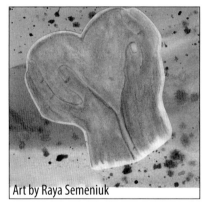

Art by Raya Semeniuk

When they arrived at the hospital, the nurse informed them that the doctor was not able to come in and they had to postpone the surgery. The friends who had come along were thrilled that they could head back to the party, with the exception of my father and his friend who felt sorry that the cousin now had to wait longer for his surgery. But just as they were ready to leave, the Mother Superior, who was the nun in charge of the hospital at the time, spoke a few quiet words to the group.

"There is a poor lady here who cannot afford to buy blood and has nobody to donate it for her. Her health is fading," was all she said. My father instinctively said he would donate his blood without thinking twice or caring that no one else volunteered to help this stranger. The others were disappointed because that meant they had to wait longer before they could go back to the party. It didn't faze my father that as a consequence he wouldn't be able to celebrate that night. There was someone in a difficult situation and he was able to help. By sharing his blood, he was giving life to this frail old woman.

The Mother Superior was so touched by his gesture of kindness to a person he had never met that she promised she would pray for him and his well-being.

To this day, my father is still proud of what he did, and I am proud of him too.

In a group of small people, he was a bigger man and put another person first by helping someone in her hour of need. Many years later, that one day still affects him deeply. To him, it was a small thing in the larger scheme of life, but to someone else, it was the gift of life.

When no one else stepped forward, he showed that true and genuine compassion comes from within. It is not something bought or acquired, it is something that stays with you and teaches you valuable lessons. It may be only a baby step or it may be a great leap, even a leap between life and death.

Allison Gonzáles

The Copper Catcher

It was always at lunchtime when a certain boy got bullied by a certain group of boys for collecting worthless pieces of round copper. It became a ritual that began in grade eight and went on until graduation day.

It was a fun game for the popular boys who threw pennies at him. He seemed to be a freak, an oddball and his name became the "Copper Catcher" because he would jump, dive, climb, and in some instances even throw himself to the ground to catch the pennies that were thrown to him. He was almost as excited as a dog fetching a stick for its master. The only difference was that this "master" did not want the stick back. It did not seem to faze him that the kids laughed at him. He was happy that he got the pennies in the end. It wasn't rare even for a teacher to hand him their extra change.

This boy seemed to be the most predictable boy in the school. Every person in every grade knew his daily routines even though most of them hadn't exchanged as much as a word with him. He would arrive at school with his home-made lunch before the teachers began to arrive. He would then attend his morning classes, catch a few pennies to fill his pockets, attend his afternoon classes and then hurry off to work. He worked in a popular corner store as a clerk, stock boy and janitor.

After graduation everyone went off to go to college or university or begin their grand careers, but the boy remained. Over the years he grew up and became the owner of the store he had been working in since grade eight. Everyone knew his routine. Even if they didn't go into the store, they would see his bike there by daybreak. He would do his morning clean up and then attend to customers and the store during the day. After closing up, he would pack up and go home.

Sometimes grown men come back to the place they grew up in when their plans of a grand life had not worked out as planned. This was a small town and there weren't many well-paying jobs around. All the good positions had been filled by people years before the Copper Catcher or any of the other kids had been out of school. Now, many of the cool kids were not so cool as men. They had come back home and they needed jobs. There was one job available that stood out as the best, but that job involved working for the freak, the multi-tasking oddball they had tormented as boys. Prepared to be shamed, each of the men walked into the store with their heads hung low, to ask for a job.

One by one, they were all enlightened and taught one of the biggest lessons of their lives. When they entered the store to ask for work, they were not met by harsh words or insults, but by kind words, as well as a job. When questioned about his decision, the Copper Catcher, now better known as Pete Sanders, would simply look up with a grin on his narrow face and respond that it was an honour to work with people that had made it possible for him to buy his store with a bunch of pennies. They had taught him that nothing is worthless. And he was simply happy to be able to repay them for all they had done for him.

It was always at lunch time that a certain man sat around the table with a certain group of men from his past, and instead of collecting pennies, they exchanged valuable ideas for the future. Because this was how they were going to move forward.

Allison Ashdown-Stone
Tattered Little Angel

Photo by
Shaylene
Charleson

When I was three years old, I was a very happy little girl; I was a bit fussy though. I would only eat purple food, wear purple clothes and read purple books. As you can see, I was a very picky, happy little girl. Even though I was happy, this was a very sad time for my mom, dad and me because my grandmother was sick and dying. She was a wonderful grandmother and I felt like I was just getting to know her. She was very tall and elegant. Even though she was quite old, her skin was very soft. I loved the way she threw her long arms around me and gave me big, loving hugs. Her hugs made me feel very safe, like no one could touch me. My grandma always wore an apron when she was in her kitchen and she hung her glasses in her shirt.

My mom was very sad over the fact that grandma was going to pass away. Grandma was as good a mom as she was a grandma. And believe me, she was a great grandma. She cheered me up when I was sad, she fed me cookies when I was hungry. She did all the great things that a grandma should, and more. The sad thing was, she smoked a lot. That was why she was dying.

When she smoked, it made my mom very sad, because she knew that she only had a few more days with grandma. Mom wanted to make the best of it! She spent every waking moment with her. Even when my grandma would lose her temper, my mom was still there right beside her. My mom and grandma were very close. When my mom was just six years old, she was diagnosed with a common disease: diabetes. Because of this, my mom and grandma had a special bond. My grandma would give my mom injections to treat her disease. That made them very close. In spite the hardship, they shared quite a lot of laughs together.

In late October of 1998, my grandma was dying for sure. We had to rush her to the hospital. Everybody was very scared and emotional. Once we got to the hospital and grandma was lying down, she slowly closed her eyes and passed over to the other side. After she died, my whole family was in shock and very sad. I did not know much about it since I was only three years old. What I did know was that I missed my grandma very much.

On the day my grandmother died, I heard some whimpering from downstairs in the basement. I loved to climb stairs when I was three and I went down to investigate. And it turned out to be my mom. She was sitting on an old stool, melting into her hands, saying words that I could not quite understand. I knew she was sad about the death of my grandma. I came up to her and said: "Don't worry, Mama, grandma is still with us. Everything is going to be OK." Then I went upstairs and brought down a tattered looking angel made of straw. My grandma had given it to me, and I gave it to my mom. As soon as I handed the angel to my mom, her frown turned upside down. I am 12 years old now and I still remember giving the angel to my mom. She remembers it too.

Heather McNeill
Magic for Carol

In 2001, I met one of the most important people in my life. Carol Newman was my Brownie leader and everyone loved her. I didn't do much program work, but looking through my book one day, one of the badges caught my eye. It was the creating and performing badge. This was at the time when the first Harry Potter movie came out. Magic, my sister and I had decided, was pretty cool. When dad said we should work on some tricks and perform them, we thought the idea was great. Several weeks later, we took along a small table and some homemade props and performed our first routine. The response was incredible. Carol had been in guiding for 18 years and said she had "never seen such a great presentation and creativity of a badge." She encouraged us to perform the three-minute-routine for the other troops. After that, we were asked if we performed at birthday parties. Now, seven years later my sister Sandra and I are still doing magic and have won numerous awards.

Photo by Sandra Fossella

In 2007, an opportunity arose to thank Carol for what she had done. I was flipping through the newspaper one day when an article jumped out at me. I read through it, thinking it was just another house that was damaged by fire. Later that day I began to feel odd about what I had read. I showed the article to Sandra. She read it and looked shocked. In my quick reading, I hadn't noticed the picture underneath. There was Carol's face gazing up at me. All I could do was look at the paper. We knew this was an opportunity to help. We spent the next few weeks organizing a show that would benefit Carol and her family. On the evening of April 26, 2007, we lugged our equipment into the room where our career began. By the end of the night, we had raised almost $500 for Carol. We were delighted that it had worked and everyone else was impressed by the show. And Carol was ecstatic.

The next day I learnt about what had happened after the show. In Carol's family there are two daughters and two sons. Carol's youngest son is borderline autistic, that means he doesn't respond to much. After coming home, he had shut himself in his room. Several hours later, he came out holding a box and showed it to Carol. He put several things into the box and made them disappear. It was a small production box that he had designed and made himself. When I learnt about the effect our magic show had had on him, I was stunned.

It had taken us roughly three weeks to organize, advertise and finally produce the show. Sandra and I had spent all our spare time preparing for it, we even used time usually allotted for homework to make it work. We put a lot of effort into the show and we were rewarded. We felt we had accomplished something worth-while and we are confident that we can do it again.

Verity Adams

Birthday Presents for Uncle Lee

Bertrand Russell once said: "Fear is the main source of superstition, and one of the main sources of cruelty. To conquer fear is the beginning of wisdom", and a year ago I would have brushed this off.

Since I was ten my mother and I have had a ritual we do every year on the day of my uncle's birthday. My uncle Lee is schizophrenic; he has been so since his early teens and he is now about fifty. He rejects medication just as he has rejected the many offers of assistance from family, friends or government agencies and instead sleeps rough, eats at soup kitchens, and occasionally picks up disability payments. Lee does not beg for money, drugs, or food; instead he asks for phone cards with just enough money left on them so he can call my grandparents here in Canada. Lee has been viciously beaten, robbed, mocked and made to feel he is worthless because he lives on the street. Because of his illness, Lee has had problems with the police, and so he tries to keep out of their way. I was told about Lee at a very early age, and could never quite understand why people would hurt him just because he lived on the street and didn't think like everyone else.

When I was ten, my mother asked me if I would like to give Lee a birthday present. We went to the sock aisle of a nearby Wal-Mart and I helped her put dozens of socks into the trolley – too many for my uncle! We then drove to East Hastings. We left the car and, carrying the socks, started to walk down the street. Very soon we saw a homeless person huddled in the corner of a doorway. Approaching him, my mother took out a pair of socks; at first the man was oblivious, but she said something to him and he almost seemed to recognize her. She gave the socks to him and turned to me. Confused, I asked why she had given Lee's present to a homeless man. Smiling, my mother said that for many years she has been coming to East Hastings on Lee's birthday and handing out chocolates, socks, gloves or things like that. I still didn't

understand until she told me that once Lee had told her that he wished that someone would do something nice for him like giving him a pair of socks for his birthday. My mother had no way of sending anything to him, so instead she had started to hand out socks to homeless people on his birthday.

Each year thereafter I came with her; but even though I felt good doing it I still didn't understand the true importance of it – until last year. We had been handing out gloves for a while when we encountered a group of men. As we were about to ask if they wanted some gloves, one of them sneered at us and told us that he "didn't want any church's charity". The whole group turned to look at us, and I think that this was the scariest situation I have ever been in. As I was about to back away, my mother told them that all she wanted to do was give out some gloves to street people like her brother, who might not have the money to pay for gloves or socks. Suddenly their menacing looks softened to a look that almost resembled something like worn happiness. The man who had sneered at us took a step forward and at first I thought he would attack us. Instead he hugged my mother and started to cry. It was as if he hadn't cried in years. Another man in the group turned to me and asked how old I was. When I told him I was fourteen he looked sad and said that he wished he had given homeless people more of a chance, and hugged me. In my life I have been hugged many times, but this hug was the most meaningful of all. It was almost as if a huge weight had been lifted off his shoulders.

Now I'm fifteen and obsessed with school, friends and badminton, but that day I vowed that for the rest of my life, no matter what, I will always give out something warm to people less fortunate than I am. If I don't, then I haven't made a difference in the world. More than anything, I wish to live in a world where people like my uncle won't be thought of as scary anymore.

Photo by Becci Delacruz

Listening & Accepting

Unspoken Words

Art by Allysa Winkler

My image shows an elderly lady who looks as if she has a story in her that hasn't been heard yet. Her life has been challenging but she has a sense of humour and she's still living her life. The hand resting on her shoulder is that of a younger person, perhaps by a generation or two. The person wants to show the old woman that she is still appreciated and that her story means something and he or she is willing to listen. The heart-shaped necklace hanging from the younger person's neck symbolizes the love shared between the two people.

Fiona Yau

When There Was No Hope

"Grandma, tell me a story!" I said. I was jumping on the bed waiting impatiently for more stories about her exciting life. I added, "Tell me about your parents. You've never told me anything about them. All you've ever talked about is your great-aunt. What happened to your parents?"

I immediately knew that something was wrong. Grandma started to blink away tears. She opened her mouth to speak but no words came out. Finally she let out a big sigh and began.

"Well. This incident happened a long time ago. I was just a five-year-old girl during World War II. The Japanese marched into Hong Kong and dropped bombs on the city all day long. It was absolutely horrifying."
Tears glistened in grandma's eyes as she was speaking.

"The soldiers killed a lot of people, even babies, and raped women who were trying to get away. Gunshots, cannon fire and the detonation of bombs were heard everywhere. Hong Kong was in a state of chaos as people desperately tried to make it to safer places. I remember that we were trying to stay together as a family. But in the pandemonium of people rushing to escape, I got pushed and fell down. When I got to my feet, I couldn't find my family anywhere."

Grandma couldn't hold in the tears any longer and they were running freely down her wrinkled cheek. I was astonished by the fact that such a tragedy had befallen my family. "Oh my gosh, what happened next?"

"I didn't know what to do. I was just a little girl. So I followed the stream of people who were escaping the city. At night, I went into caves to hide or slept in grassy fields. When I got hungry, I ate tree bark. When I was thirsty, I drank from the puddles of water on the ground. That was the most dreadful month of my life. After the war had ended, everything started to get back to normal

and I returned to Hong Kong. I wandered the streets for days in search of my missing family, but I didn't have any luck at all. One day, I came to an outdoor market and sat down against a wall. I had nowhere to go. I just sat there, crying and begging for money. Just when I thought that there was no hope left for me, your great-aunt came up to me and asked if I had been separated from my family. I nodded and she offered to take care of me until I recovered my health and found my family."

At this point, grandma smiled for the first time since the start of our conversation.

"And that is why I grew up with great-aunt and not my parents. She was amazingly kind to me and treated me like her own daughter. She was the one who made me feel like I had a reason to live."

I finally found my voice and asked, "Is that why you adopted Aunt Macy?"

"Yes, because I felt like it was my duty to pass on this kind of generosity."

This story has stayed with me as a perfect example of compassion. Great-aunt saw a poor and lonely kid on the street and took care of her without hesitation. And my grandma adopted Aunt Macy, because she remembered the time when it seemed like she had no one she could turn to. Aunt Macy has been so grateful to be adopted that she also took in a young boy a couple of years ago. Thus, this one act of compassion has not only saved the life of one person, but the empathy has been passed from generation to generation.

Now I truly understand that even though there may be a lot of selfish and uncaring people in the world, there is always going to be someone who is willing to lend a hand to people in desperate need of help. The power of compassion is embedded in the human nature. All it needs is to be discovered.

Annie Chu
Would You Like Some Coffee?

When I put on my green apron, I am a new person. I leave my emotions at the door and my day starts again. I remember the first day at my job, a local café – I met this man while I was learning the register. He was my first customer. He must have been a regular because everyone around me greeted him instantly.

"Hey, Chase," they all said in unison. That was how I learned his name.

Chase was in his early twenties, had blond hair and blue eyes. He looked like a movie star, but instead worked at a construction site. He would always come in for a Quad Grande Non-fat Americano Misto after work. The first time I spoke to him, I was on my break. It was mid-morning and the café was quiet. My backpack was on the stool next to me while I sat reading. The book was open in my hands when my thoughts were interrupted by a voice.

"Hey, you like Atwood too?"

"Yeah, she's alright. I'm reading *The Blind Assassin*, I hesitantly replied. I was not used to strangers talking to me. I turned around to see who it was.

"Yeah, she's great, isn't she? I read most of her books. Hi, I'm Chase, by the way."

"Hello," I replied, shaking his outstretched hand.

"Wait, you work here, right?"

"That's what my shirt says," I replied pointing at my t-shirt that clearly displayed the café's logo, a cup surrounded by swirls.

"Well, I'll see you later." He waved his hand and left. Chase was loquacious. As time went on, I learned more about him and we became friends. When he came on weekends, I would always ask for my break, so I could talk to him. Even though he was tired from work, he was enthusiastic to tell me what was going on.

One sunny afternoon, Chase and I were sitting inhaling the earthy smell of freshly brewed coffee. I sat staring at him; he was looking down at his cup, attempting to sip

some coffee but his hand shook. After a moment, he set his cup down.

"My girlfriend's pregnant and we're getting married," he said.

His face glowed; I was speechless. I was happy for him. The first time we had a real conversation he had told me about his girlfriend, Leslie. They met in their first year of high school and she was his first serious relationship. After graduation, Chase's family moved. But Chase decided to quit school and move out to live on his own so he could be with Leslie. That was how he ended up with a construction job.

"You deserve this, Chase, you really do."

"Thanks. I'm just glad something is working out finally. I mean, I knew we were meant to be together, it's just that we're so young. But now we have something so wonderful to bring to the world and I'm so excited to hold it in my arms in nine months."

After that conversation, I noticed that Chase didn't come in for his regular coffee on the weekends anymore.

It was raining the day I saw Chase again. I was off my shift when he came in. He was wobbling and toppled over one of the chairs – he was a mess. I ran over and kneeled beside him.

"Chase, what's wrong? Why are you like this?"

"Life's a bitch and then you die," he mouthed with a heavy scent of Crown Royal.

"What happened? Is there anything I can help you with?"

He was silent for a while. I had no idea what to do next. I pulled him into on of the big armchairs and sat down next to him.

"Alright, well, you know that Leslie's pregnant, right?"

"The baby is not yours?" I asked.

"Ha, no, it's mine, but Leslie's moved."

"What? But I thought that you guys were planning to get married."

"Ha, married! Her parents shipped her off to some relatives when they found out she was pregnant. I've been calling her but there were no replies. So I went to her place and her parents told me she's gone, forever, and I must leave."

"I don't understand. Didn't you tell them that you were planning to get married?"

"Come on, look at me, I'm no Bill Gates," he said, "Actually to quote them, "I'm a poor son of a bitch that will never make it big or succeed in anything I do, and I have just ruined their daughter's life. But since she's gone, I won't ruin it further." But I mean they're taking away my baby and the love of my life. I don't know what I will do without them."

I didn't know what to say. Nothing I'd say would make him feel better, but I knew that he needed me there to listen to him. Why else would he come here? He continued for another few minutes, telling me how he tried looking for her and how devastated he was. Finally he stopped and sat back in the purple velvet armchair. He brought his hands up towards his face and buried it there.

"I know, you must be wondering why I came here, of all the places, right?" he asked after a minute or so. "Well, a lot of people didn't accept me and Leslie. She was my sweetheart, but a lot of people couldn't stand her. All my friends thought I could do better. So if I went to them, they'd be happy. Also, there is one more reason…"

"What is it?" I asked.

"Because I knew you would listen."

"Aw, Chase, you must hang in there. Don't stop doing whatever you think is right."

"I know, thanks for reminding me." His mouth curved slightly upwards, as if he was trying to smile but couldn't.

"You know where to find me if anything." I said.

"Thanks." He got up and moved towards the door. His fingers brushed the cold door handle and stopped for a second. He looked back at me and smiled, a real smile, and then he pushed through the door and left. The cold breeze rushed in, sending chills down my back. I leaned back in my chair.

"Good luck, Chase."

Photo by Becci Delacruz

Sami Low

A Sunday Afternoon

Glancing up at the building, I shiver and clench my hands as I clamber out of the car. Even though the sun is shining, the air is still quite cold and I realize that I should have brought a jacket. My eyes travel along the length of the wooden panels from one dilapidated window to the next. Most of the curtains are drawn, though one or two are not.

Walking towards the sliding doors, I pass underneath a large red gateway erected above the entrance. I crane my head to see the gold writing etched into the wood, though it is written in Chinese and I can't read it. Ornate dragons decorate the panel and the border shows an intricate design that runs the length of all sides. The doors open with a whoosh as I step inside, thankful for the warm air. A small bronze statue, displayed on the opposite wall, greets me. Walking closer I realize that it is the head of the founder of the care home.

I follow my mom down the hallway until we stop in front of an elevator where she pushes the "up" button. I can hear the various parts clanking and whirring behind the wall and I know it will take a little while for the elevator to open. I look over my shoulder to gaze down a long corridor with several doors. Most of them are open and there is a trolley stacked high with towels and an assortment of clothes pushed up against the wall.

A lady walks out of a room, pushing an elderly man in a wheelchair. He is small and fragile; his skin is wrinkled and aged. He puts his head in his hands as he is led to the back of a queue where other elderly people have been lined up, all of them in wheelchairs. One lady yells loudly, as if she was trying to say something and a nurse hurries to her side and leads her away, down the hallway. "They're going for their dinner," my mother explains when she notices what I'm looking at. I nod and then the doors open, admitting us into the elevator. I lean against the rail until my mom gives me a disapproving look that tells me I have done something wrong. "Don't lean against the rail, it's dirty," she says.

I sigh and step away as the elevator shudders and comes to a stop.

"Her room is 207, this way." We walk past a large living room where I see people sitting around a television set. Some of the occupants are in wheelchairs while others hold onto canes and walkers. A few are watching the show, but most of them have fallen asleep. We pass a small counter where two women are typing away at a computer. They smile as we walk by. When we enter a smaller hallway, I begin counting the numbers as we pass each door: 201…203…205…207.

Mrs. Mow Jun Wong, the nameplate says and above it are the Chinese characters. The door is slightly ajar and I can hear sounds coming from inside as my mom pushes it open and we walk into the room. My grandma is sitting on a chair facing her dresser and adjusting the volume of a handheld radio. She looks up as we enter. She is wearing her favourite tan hat and four layers of clothing. My mother took her shopping a few weeks ago and I can see that she is wearing the new brown top we bought for her. She has buttoned it up to her neck, but not the bottom part.

I wave, "Hi Popo!" She grins broadly, waving her hands and nodding her head.

"Hi, hi," she says in strongly accentuated English. My grandma is an interesting lady. She just turned ninety, yet she is in good health and hasn't lost her mobility, though she uses a walker. She hoards food and napkins in her drawers, much to my mom's dismay, as she always ends up having to empty them out. The nurses say that this is a common habit among the elderly, and that a lot of residents in the care home do it.

"Hi Mom," my mother shouts loudly over the radio, "what are you doing?" They continue to converse, though it is difficult for me to follow as they have slipped into the Chinese dialect of my grandma's small village. Looking around the room, I see a vase of pink roses on the dresser, along with various cards and pictures. I see myself in one photo and I smile at the cards we wrote for her.

"She likes the flowers," my mom tells me. "She says they make the room smell good." Popo is rummaging through her dresser now. Her room is very small, so it tends to get cluttered easily. She often puts something down and later forgets its location. So I look apprehensive as she pulls out a bag of candies and gestures at us.

"Ley yew?" (You want?) My mom shakes her head, "No, no. Let's go downstairs."

There's a little sitting area downstairs with sofas and plants, and a garden outside that we like to walk in. Unlike most of the other residents, my grandma is actually quite plump and my mom says that she has gained weight since moving here. We like to get her out of her room and walk around with her when we visit. Grandma asks one last time, lifting up the candy bag. I shake my head and she laughs before putting it back into the drawer and looking for her shoes. I follow my mom out of the room and we pace the hallway. Popo takes a while getting ready. She insists on bringing a purse with her and then she has to turn back to close the window before she leaves.

"Hurry up, we're leaving." My mom shouts and she rolls her eyes at me, but she is smiling a little.

"Look at the flowers." Popo says pointing at them. We are outside in the garden and I watch as my grandma shuffles by the flowers, admiring their colours and showing us the ones she particularly likes. Two sparrows perch on a tree branch and I watch as she catches sigh of them. She talks excitedly, following them with her finger as they hop around and then fly off, into the sky.

Inside, the sunlight shines through the glass windows and the room is light and spacious. My grandma makes her way to the potted orange tree and I notice little red tags hanging from the branches. They have Chinese characters written on them. Popo is talking excitedly now, not seeming to notice that we haven't said anything for a while. She touches the cards and then she turns to me and reads them out for me. "This one is funny," my mother says. "It translates to big laugh."

I smile and Popo laughs, pointing again. We sit on one of the sofas and Popo talks more with my mom interjecting with "Oh, really" and "Good, good." My grandma enjoys it when we come to see her and she's almost always in a happy, talkative mood. She gets bored at the care home sometimes, so she looks forward to our visits. She turns to me suddenly and I know by her inquiring tone that she is asking me a question. I nod at her and smile, but it is a sad smile. It saddens me that despite three years of Chinese school, I am only a little more literate than when I first started. I feel a twinge of regret that I didn't make more of an effort to learn my native tongue, that my younger self thought it more of a chore than a learning experience. I saw it as just another class I had to drag myself through. Now, as I sit next to Popo, I realize how much I've missed out. Popo asks again, surprisingly patient.

And my mother steps in, "She asks how old you are. She can't remember."

"Sixteen." I respond in shaky Chinese. I have to say the numbers from one to sixteen in my head before I can answer, because I can't quite remember them individually. I feel like a toddler who is just learning the alphabet.

"Good, good." My grandma nods approvingly. I sink back into the sofa, stare at the ceiling and notice a cobweb in the corner. I cannot imagine how my grandma must feel to be in a foreign country, or talking to me. Was she upset? Disappointed? Either way, I'm glad that although I cannot talk easily with her, I can still enjoy her company and spend time with her. My mom glances at her watch. "We should get going. It's getting late." She turns to grandma who is sitting contentedly on the sofa and tells her that we need to leave.

Popo nods, "Okay, okay. Bye bye."

We walk towards the foyer and I stand beside Popo as she shuffles along with her walker. My mom cut two tennis balls and put them on the legs of the walker so that it would be easier to push. She said that it would glide more easily on the floor like this.

"You can take the elevator by yourself?" my mom asks. Popo nods her head and waves her hand in an ushering motion. "Go on," she is saying.

"Bye Popo!" I say as we walk through the sliding door outside.

Photography by Karen San

Old Chairs on the Porch

When I saw this house, I had a feeling that a lonely old person inhabited it. On the porch, there are some old chairs that look like they've been left out waiting for someone to sit on. But in the end, all that was put on top were some rags and a bottle. It reminds me of compassion because it seems like no one ever came to visit. The person living here must have been so lonely. And I almost feel like I want to go sit on the chairs and liven up the scene.

Photography by Nikita Morgan

The Nest

It once was nothing but scattered sticks on the ground. They were specially chosen by a bird that made them a part of its home. The nest is strong; it is made to last. The bird may have flown away to start over somewhere else. And the nest was left abandoned, maybe it will become another bird's home?

Carmen Lee
Table Tennis

Donating hundreds of dollars to a charity, giving away priceless gifts or throwing an expensive surprise party for a friend are all acts of human kindness and are excellent ways of showing your appreciation to someone. But most of us aren't movie stars who can afford to give away such things. Acts of kindness, therefore, can take many different shapes and forms. Holding open a door, supporting a friend or comforting a sad person are just a number of ways to show how much you care. With a cumulating effect, small acts of kindness done daily will bring joy into many people's lives.

Photo by Becci Delacruz

When one feels down, the best way to make them feel better is through your support. One word, a comment or just a warm smile will immediately show them that you care. The kindness received by the person is like the warmth you feel when the sun shines brightly. I am very fortunate to have experienced this power of kindness.

I play table tennis and during one trip to compete in a championship, I was playing very poorly but a few encouraging words spoken to me turned around my approach for the remaining matches.

"I saw you play and you're a pretty good player. Just because you lost to someone who is younger than you, that doesn't mean that you have to lose all your confidence," he stated.

"Yes, I know," I replied, "but it's just difficult to accept that."

"You have to find the fire inside. And forget about everything else except the fact that you have to play to your best ability and nothing else will matter," he said.

He left me thinking about those remarks that later led me to a great victory. At the end of the day, I was able to compete again with the player who I had previously lost to. After hearing those comments, I played in a different way – with more confidence than before. I tried not to care too much about the score, but played the best way I could. Thus I won the game because I was more relaxed. During the whole match, I received support and applause from the same person who had had the discussion with me earlier. I was very thankful because I realized that through this support I was able to clear my mind. By not thinking that I was definitely going to lose, I played much better.

The odd thing is that my supporter was a total stranger. He just came up to me and told me about his observations. This showed me that some people are considerate enough to support you even though they have no idea who you are. And I was grateful to that person for taking the time to encourage me.

Acts of kindness come in small packages or huge gifts. They may or may not affect people in a big way, but they will definitely leave an impact. Kindness brightens the day for everyone. Without it, we live in a cloudy atmosphere waiting for the sun to break through. It only takes a little bit of your time to make someone believe they can accomplish something – and with that encouragement obstacles can disappear right in front of your eyes.

Photo by Brenda De Vera

Jackson Nerland

Are You Okay?

I remember what happened that year. I had hoped that grade six, a new year at elementary school, would be filled with fun and excitement. But I was wrong. I sat there, my nose running, their scornful words replaying in my head. Not caring what anyone thought, I wept openly and tears were staining my cheeks. I hated this, hated their disapproval.

They had invited me to play football, a rare occurrence, and I had accepted. We started playing and it turned out that I wasn't half bad. But then I fumbled the ball. You would think that this was just a forgivable mistake – it wasn't like I was the only one who had failed a pass. But this incident set them off; it was all it took for them to turn on me. Again. As always, they were the hounds while I was the fox. Insults were hurled at me. And I heard them all. But one comment had the power to hurt me the most because it came from someone I had considered to be a friend. Riled by the mob, he walked up to me and shouted, "To think that we invited you to play. It is so like you to just screw up. But then again, what's new? You were never any good at sports." That was all it took to shatter me. I ran away to hide from them, to hide my pain.

And then she came along. She came out of nowhere, her feature were blurred by my tears. She offered me a Kleenex and asked if I was okay. After wiping my teary eyes, I noticed that she had blond hair and a tough look: a straight nose, a jutting chin and high cheekbones. But those hard features were softened by the empathy that radiated from her. She stayed with me for a while, in silence, but this was all I needed. Just her presence calmed me and brought some happiness. She asked me once again if I was alright, and I nodded my head in acknowledgement. She decided to leave and said she hoped that everything was okay.

I never found out who she was. I passed her in the hall occasionally, but I never mustered the courage to ask what her name was. And when the next year of school arrived, she wasn't there. After finishing my grade seven year, I thought that I might run into her at high school, but I didn't. I never saw her again but her kindness never left me and I will always be thankful that she stopped to see if I was okay. It was this small act of compassion that helped me, not just this once, but though all the rough times to come.

Photo by Becci Delacruz

Howard Lee

I Understand

It was near the end of the school year, the busiest time of the year. Dark winter nights had long given way to sweat-inducing summer days. The continuous tick-tick of the rain had been replaced by the cheerful chirping of the birds and in this blissful heaven, there was a dark smudge. That smudge was me and I was mad – mad at life.

It seemed to me that the whole world was falling apart like a vanilla-chocolate ice cream cone in the summer heat, melting and melting until it turns into a puddle of swirling brown and white. My grade spiraled down through a wormhole into another dimension full of agitated moms and blue-faced teachers. Physically I improved only by a miniscule five centimeters in high jump from my score two years before. And my coach had long given up on me succeeding in competitive swimming. On the softer side, I barely scraped through leading the second violins in the senior orchestra, let alone impressing a panel of adjudicators in an audition; and the violin exam was coming up. To top at all off, the girl I loved didn't talk to me much.

All in all, I was frustrated with life. Very frustrated. I started to have mood swings. When the pendulum swung to the left, I was as irritable as a rhino and when it swung to the right, I would drown in a turbulent sea of misery. Some of my friends noticed and left like bees in search for better nectar, others cared out of politeness. Few sincerely wanted to help. Soon I was excluded from hang-outs and gossip. I started avoiding certain people and lashing out at others. I tried to skip both the swim and track practices and holed up in my room pretending to be asleep with my earphones blaring, ignoring my mom's daily dose of lectures.

I knew that needed to talk to someone before I imploded, but the words just wouldn't come out. An armour of happiness had protected my inner self faithfully over so many years, yet I could feel it slowly deteriorating from this corrosive assault. It left me vulnerable and I noticed how people I didn't usually talk to would laugh about me and taunt me behind my back.

Finally a loyal friend came up to me and said, "Hey, you want to talk? All these things you've got going on 'n stuff…I don't think I can help much, but…" He helped more than he thought. The dam burst and everything flooded out.

After talking to him, as I was slowly walking back home, I almost cried from the relief of being able to share this burden with a person I trusted, and in knowing that somebody out there cared about me. Finally I was able to pull myself back together and started to patch things up. All I can really say is, "Thank you."

Su Lin

By My Side

Photo by Mitchelle Torres

Self-portrait

This picture shows a woman who is very emotional. She seems broken-hearted or sad because she has been left behind. I know that this sad girl is looking for compassion and help. But I don't know if I can help, because she is me.

My childhood had cast a huge shadow over me because there were many obstacles, like stress and depression, blocking my happiness. Gradually I became tired of my life and lost trust in others. I felt that I had caged myself in a transparent glass tower, where I could see what other people were doing, but I could not get out. This was my comfort zone, I was afraid of stepping out, but it was also suffocating me. When I was clinging to a sliver of hope, standing at the last corner, a girl came into my life. At first I hated her for her happiness, openness and enthusiasm. Although she was not perfect, I wished to be her because she seemed to have everything I did not possess. Her name was Jenny.

When I was in grade nine, I applied for the International Baccalaureate program at school, a program I longed to join. Unfortunately, I was rejected. But Jenny was accepted. My failure tortured me for so long that despised myself. A year later, I had another chance to apply. This time, I hesitated. I was afraid to fail again because that would have been like sprinkling salt on a cut. I was struggling with the decision when Jenny offered to help. She told me that I could do this as long as I believed in myself. During one of my toughest times, she was by my side, giving me advice. When the time for the entrance exam came, she brought me to see my previous English teacher, one of my favourite teachers, to cheer me up. What touched me the most was that Jenny was very busy at that time, and she had a lot of homework and projects. However, she did not refuse to help me. For the first time in my life, I felt so grateful for having a friend. I finally cried my heart out after all the years of suppressed emotions. I shed all the grudges with my tears. And all the sorrow I had hidden deep inside me was washed away.

Gradually, I joined more school activities, and stayed in my room less. Now, when I see some students sitting quietly in the corner, I will try to talk to them. They may be like me, tired of life because they have no real friends. Jenny has taught me to be empathetic, and willing to trust and understand others. Empathy is not necessarily something big and significant, but when you are willing to try to help other people, you will give them a lot of hope, courage, and confidence. If everyone tries to help at least one person, the world will be a much better place with less depression and sorrow.

Tanisha Salomons

I've Been There

In December 2005, Grant, one of my best friends, was diagnosed with lymphoma. His sudden diagnosis caused him to withdraw from most of his friends and family; he felt alone in dealing with his disease. He went from being a healthy, strong teenager to someone who gradually lost his hair as he sat in a clinic receiving chemotherapy. None of his doctors seemed to understand the pain he was going through. None of his friends were able to comprehend the fact that most of the time, he wanted to give up.

One day, Grant turned to me in an effort to simply vent about what he was experiencing and through this I discovered my ability to empathize. For the first time in my life, I found that I could help somebody simply by being able to relate. I had been sick for three years and although I didn't have cancer, I experienced many of the same things Grant experienced. I too was unable to attend school, be around friends, or lead a normal life. I had been forced to give up most of what was familiar to me as a result of something beyond my control. But I made it through. And by being able to tell Grant that I'd been there, that I have faced many of the same struggles he was going through, I was able to give him something more valuable than his numerous doctors had been able to provide him with. By knowing that I thoroughly understood what he was telling me, he, for the first time since his diagnosis, felt less alone.

Compassion is not so much about the material things you can give to a person, but rather about giving all that you are able to give. Although I am not able to cure Grant's cancer or ease his physical pain, I can be there for him. Being there for him when he needs it, be it by staying up all hours until the morning talking with him, or writing to him, or making up songs with him, makes his days a little easier and that knowledge is enough reason for me to do it.

Compassion requires a certain amount of sacrifice. It is more than sympathy, more than feeling pity for someone. It also goes beyond empathy, beyond being able to relate to someone's experiences as your own. Compassion adds to those qualities the desire to relieve another person's suffering. Compassion also has the intrinsic hidden quality of being reciprocal. When one person extends compassion to another and tries to alleviate that person's hardship, they often find, unexpectedly, that they receive something even greater in return. My own illness and how it affected my life remain difficult issues even now that I am better: the things I missed when I was ill, the pain I went through, the loneliness. I still resent thinking or speaking about this. Talking with Grant about my own experiences opened wounds that I had thought were healed and I've come to realize that I had simply covered them up. Sharing my story with Grant was painful for me, but by my showing my vulnerability, he was able to take my words for their true value. I found that in showing compassion to Grant, I took a big step toward healing myself.

Brendan Grist

Kindness

A long time ago there was a beautiful maiden named Kindness. Her hair shone as if it was lacquered. Her lips were painted with gentle words and had a sweet look to them. Her eyes took in any tragedies no matter how great and her cheeks were soft and full, ready to hold the world's sorrow and tears. But it was not only her face that was beautiful, her body was long and lean as well as strong. Her feet never touched the ground, only toeing it gently so as not to take anything away that another person might enjoy. Her father's name was Any Person. Any Person needed Kindness, for his life was not good to him and Kindness was the only thing that made it better. She gave all she had to Any Person. Each day she worked hard to please Any Person and make him happy and only after doing that was she happy herself.

Art by Ella Moynihan

The news of her tremendous beauty spread to every corner of the earth. One day it reached the kingdom called Hardship. Hardship was an anguished kingdom. All living there had lost something; all felt they had nothing to hope for. The people's faces were drawn with the things they'd seen and the people they'd lost. The land's king was named Hunger. He was a restless king and never happy with what he had. He wanted Kindness for himself so much that he went all the way to Kindness' house to bring her back to his kingdom without a thought of Any Person.

When Kindness came to Hunger's Kingdom of Hardships, she saw the dead look in people's eyes. But she did not turn away, because every person needs to see Kindness first to learn from her. Their eyes hungrily drank in this beauty; all of them wanted something to hope for and she looked like she could give it to them. She stepped onto a pedestal before the people. Looking at them, she filled up with such hope and good intentions that they almost came spilling out of her mouth. She wanted to change the lives of the people in Hardship, so she began.

A wind moved her hair, wrapping around her face like soft silken feathers. The people all sighed at its beauty. She then, without a single word, pulled out a thin silver sword and with one savage slice, cut off her hair and let it fall down onto the people's heads, quickly becoming part of their hair and making them beautiful as well. The people were puzzled. No one had asked her to do this and she was not getting anything in return. As the people looked at Kindness, they all thought she looked less than what she was before. She stepped down from her pedestal and stood with the people. She then kissed every person, giving them her kind words and taking their sorrow upon her back and became stooped under its great weight. The bitter taste of their tears was now on her cracked lips.

When she was done, her beauty was gone and all the people left her, for what more could she give them? But Kindness smiled, for her beauty was now something everyone had.

Kindness quietly left Hunger's Kingdom of Hardship and went back to her home with Any Person. Any Person was overjoyed, throwing his hands up in the air. He was happy with the little beauty that was left in Kindness, whatever her form.

Bryce Balcom

Butterfly Effect

On a spring day, a few of my friends and I were wandering down Yonge Street in Toronto. We were coming from a model UN conference so we looked very conspicuous in our business attire. We came across an arcade and went inside. After a few minutes, two of my friends and I decided to continue further down Yonge Street. Before leaving, I took out my wallet to give those of my friends who were remaining at the arcade a few quarters. As I walked to the entrance of the arcade, I was tapped on the shoulder. Turning around, I saw an elderly gentleman. He had stopped to hand me the wallet that I had dropped. In the hustle and bustle of the arcade I had not noticed that it had fallen out of my pocket. His attire of shabby clothes contrasted sharply with my business attire. This man who, by all appearances, needed the money far more than I, decided to give back my wallet. His only possible reason was that he believed it was the right thing to do. A few hours later when I returned to the arcade I saw that he was handing out slips of paper about Christ. His generosity had piqued my interest and I asked for one.

I am an atheist. Regardless of my personal belief towards religion, I can see that the man acted the way he did out of compassion. He believed that he was helping the people he encountered. It doesn't matter what you believe in. It simply matters that you act out of compassion, out of kindness. Jesus was not the first person to advocate for compassion but he was one of the most successful. The basis of the Christian religion, once you strip off all the supernatural and miracles, are the ideas of community and compassion. This is an idea we can all relate to. The Christian religion and others like it have been promoting basic human values for eons. Jesus' act of compassion spurred others to act compassionately. Every time someone is treated with compassion, they are inspired to help others. A single act of compassion affects those it touches and instills a desire to be compassionate. This is the fabled butterfly effect in action.

The idea of the butterfly effect is that when a single butterfly flaps its wings, a tornado is created on the other side of the world. Thus a single small act can change the world. When the butterfly flaps its wings, it pushes the air with its wings. The air it moves goes on to move more air that, in turn, goes on to move more air. Through this, a gust of wind too small to feel becomes one that can lift houses.

Compassion is itself an act of faith – faith in your fellow human beings to carry the torch. You have no way of knowing that the people following after you in the chain will act as you have. You can only act as you hope others will act and eventually you will make the world better, whether you can measure it or not. We can connect with other nations – not with war or government-to-government talks – but with simple kindness.

Let me give you an example. A young man named Tsering came to Mulgrave School, the school I attend, from Tibet because of the compassion and kindness of a man named Peter Dalglish. Peter Dalglish is a humanitarian currently working in Tibet. When he met Tsering he put great effort into finding a home and a school for Tsering. Mulgrave has a history of taking in exchange students until they graduate. This aid, this act of compassion has helped Tsering get to where he is and has also encouraged him to help others. And the people he helps will also be inspired to act compassionately. It can spread like wildfire and burn this idea of compassion into the minds of everyone it touches.

I stand here today moved by the action of compassion that the man at the arcade has shown me. I'm motivated to make a difference in someone else's life just as he affected mine. That man had no idea what effect would come from his act of kindness and nor do I.

I simply carry the torch.

Emily Snee

Ripples

It can be shown so easily, so simply
And yet it is such an unattainable feeling
It ripples through us
In rings of time
Forming circles of inclusion
That widen as more people feel
The effects
Of the stone dropped

So easily ignored
So easily unseen
And so rarely acknowledged

And yet it could be so simple
Something easy to do
That has so much impact
Holds so much worth

Fingertips intended tenderly
Brushing across your knuckles
A comforting whisper
Tickling and hissing into your left ear
The sweet, fresh mint
Of tic-tacs given to you by a friend
Melting over your garlic-tainted tongue
The forgiving and understanding smile
Of an old friend, turned enemy
The homely scent of baking
Wafting in from a kitchen called
'Apology'

Perhaps even something as easy as
"How are you?"

Or

"Are you okay?"

These simple things
So easily ignored
Passed over and accepted
Without another thought

Part of nature
Just like ripples pushing out

As basic as

Opening arms
Grabbing and pulling you into a warm
embrace

So underrated
And so often
Overlooked

But the warmth of a hug
That warmth of body
Shows a warmth of heart
A warmth of intentions
A warmth like
Standing by a river
Under the summer sun
Sweltering
And loving
The sweat pouring down
Your neck and back

A warmth like
Second degree burns
From pushing your
Wood filled hands
Into dying flames
And pulling
Hot, jumping sparks into the air

Surrounding your fingers
Intense
With the heat of practicality

A warmth like
No other
As intense as
The cold you feel
Pushing through your body
When you stand
On the beach
As the moon begins pulling in
A dusty blanket of darkness
Throwing your arms out
To accept the stars above you
Telling them
You don't mind that they're cold
Because you have enough warmth
Not in your body
But in your mind
In your soul
In your heart
And in your intentions
To heat this world
This universe
For an eternity

It can be shown so easily, so simply and
yet
It is such an unattainable feeling
It ripples through us
In rings of time
Forming circles of inclusion
That widen as more people feel
The effects
Of the stone
Dropped

Art by Brianna Forbes-Crowe

Kit Sauder

Making Strangers Smile

Art by Aaron Lao

I live in a town with beautiful sunsets. The sea comes up and caresses the coast and the sun sinks over the mountains across the ocean. I live in a town where almost everyone has almost every material thing they want. I live in a town where people have forgotten to watch the sun go down.

I've spent a lot of my life dealing with grief. Mostly my own, grief I do not and will not dwell on. From the experience I have learnt to appreciate the sunsets in my perfect little town. Despite our privileged lives I have discovered that many people who live and work and love alongside each other, are very unhappy.

I am an actor, and on my way home from a rehearsal some months ago, I saw a woman sitting on a hill crying. I kept walking, thinking to myself, "Why isn't anyone there to hold her?" I got about a block away, turned around and walked back up the hill. She was clearly upset and like most people, ashamed of it. As I approached she watched me warily and said, "You walked all the way up that hill for me?"

I merely grinned and told her that one should never sit alone too long when crying. I never got her name. I never asked. It didn't seem something important. I never learned what was bothering her either. She told me she had grown up here; that she hadn't swum in the ocean in thirty years. She had brown hair and tired eyes and skin darkened by the sun. By the end of the conversation she had laughed, and we had both cried.

I walked home content. That afternoon I bore witness to the life of a stranger. I had helped her to smile and I had gained nothing from it, nothing material anyway. It is surprising that one can give so little and have such a large impact. I don't know her name. I hope she swam in the ocean that day.

Art by Rebecca Shaw

Action-Courage-Hope

Art by Aya Tubinshlak

My picture symbolizes a number of things. The red splatters in the background symbolize blood or dispute. The two hands stretching out to one another symbolize pushing past all that dispute and coming together. The olive tree and the dove holding the olive branch symbolize peace, freedom, and most importantly, hope.

Flora Yu

Why Pink?

Praises I longed for, didn't arise,

Teases anxiously waited for each sun to rise.

By the school door was where he stood,

His ghastly face hidden behind his hood.

A punch, a kick and even a word,

It's always the same for what just occurred,

Marked bruises and cratered scars,

Forever etched on a hurting heart.

I ran, I screamed, I pleaded for peace,

But nothing at all seemed to please.

Colours soon began to fade,

Arriving at a tunnel of deep grey,

A world of darkness and nothing more,

Definitely not worth living for.

Object in hand, ready to slit,

But, a light suddenly shines up this pit,

Blinding indeed, but giving guidance,

A hand emerges for assistance.

Helped up into a new position,

Freed from the bully's ambition,

I shall never conceal myself again,

Instead, let's form a nationwide chain.

I wear pink, you wear pink,

From now on, bullying shall sink!

Irene Hong

Bully

Although tolerance of different races is a concept that is taught to today's children, many are incapable of grasping such a obscure and mature idea. Because of this lapse in understanding, many children are subjected to ridicule and humiliation arising from the colour of their skin. I was a victim of such a misunderstanding a number of years ago, and even though the pain I experienced seemed unbearable, I can now appreciate the experience and what it has taught me.

I had been raised in the Western culture since I was four years old, and have always considered myself as part of the status quo, even though it was undeniable that I was not Caucasian, but Asian. This difference had not bothered me a great deal as my peers had accepted me. I remember the first instance of derogatory racial comments directed at me when I was only about six years old. Some of the older children had devised a clever chant in which they sang "Chinese, Japanese, Koreaaan" while manipulating their eyes so that they were barely visible slits. At the time I had not quite understood what this meant, but I knew I was being teased about my heritage. Soon after, these older children found out my real Asian name and proceeded to pronounce it as incorrectly as possible on purpose. They laughed hysterically after each outrageous pronunciation. After this incident I made sure that no one would know my Asian name until they had earned my trust.

I quickly moved past this unpleasant memory and received no further racial belittlement until the sixth grade. In this awkward stage of puberty, acceptance meant everything. I had already been suffering from low self-esteem, as many adolescents at this stage do, when one of my classmates decided that my difference was something worthy of derision. Being one out of four Asian students in my grade, it was obvious that I was part of a minority. My bully started slowly and first teased me about the Asian food I frequently brought for lunch.

"Ugh, what is that SMELL?" he posed the question loudly and swiveled his head around searching for the source of his disdain. Everyone quickly glanced down at his or her lunch to check if it was offensive in any way.

"God, Irene, what is that?" he shrieked, pointing at the stir-fry rice I had been eating. My face turned scarlet as everyone turned to look at me. He continued to ask about my food and why it smelled so "funky." My friends did nothing to help me; they all gazed at my now strange and unappealing meal. After that day, I refused to take any form of Asian food to school and ordered my mother to pack what was deemed as normal Caucasian foods. Unfortunately, my bully didn't give up. He saw my change in meals as a sign of defeat and an invitation to further ridicule. He proceeded to call me by "fun nicknames" as he termed them, like "1-800-Chow-Mein" or "Chinky Hongster." He would mimic Asian accents even though I did not have one. This continuous abuse to my heritage caused me to loathe it with a passion. Why couldn't I be "normal"? Why couldn't I be like everyone else? I asked myself these questions daily while enduring verbal torture from him.

I wasn't able to answer those questions until years later. As time passed, maturity allowed me to accept who I was. I was normal and there was nothing wrong with me. On the contrary, I had been blessed with the background of another culture that gave me a broader and more open-minded perspective of life. One day, I came upon a scene where an Asian student was being teased for her race. I did not know the student, but I immediately jumped in and confronted the antagonist. Afterwards the student thanked me for standing up for her. As she wiped tears from her eyes, she looked at me for a long time.

"Why did you help me, you don't even know me?" She asked. "Because I know what it feels like," I replied. It was then that it hit me – the full potential of the power compassion can hold. Compassion from one person can alleviate another's pain. This made me realize what could be achieved if everyone could experience such a poignant emotion. The result would be worldwide harmony.

Jany Gao

The Cobbler

It was a summer day many years ago in the sun-baked city of Nanjing, China.

The story had a shaky but inconspicuous beginning: my parent had some pressing business to attend to and I had to go to my piano lesson on my own. I was unhappy, but not concerned. I had traveled through the city by myself before and thought there was no problem. But there was. First I boarded the wrong bus and ended up in an unknown part of the city. Then I lost the little money I had in the mad scramble to retrace my steps. Finally, as if to complete the circle of misfortune, the straps on my right sandal snapped.

So there I was, holding my broken sandal in a nameless alley, lost and stunned. People passed by, some spared a look, but they were all gone within a blink. I hung my head and was about to cry when I heard a voice beside me.

"Little girl, are you alright?"

Startled, I looked up. Standing next to me was a man of about forty years, with an ordinary face and very black eyes. He wore a rough cotton shift and a blue apron on top. A grimy tea towel of undistinguishable colour was thrown over his shoulder.

"Are you okay?" he asked. "What's the matter, little girl?"

"My sandal is broken," I sniffed.

His face broke into a grin.

"Well, that's no problem. I'm a cobbler. In a few minutes I'll have your sandal as good as new."

He led me to the sidewalk where he had set up his booth under a blooming tree. There was a large toolbox filled to the brim and a few stools scattered about.

"Sit, sit," he said, pointing to a stool while sitting down on another one himself. "It will take just a few minutes."

I sat down and blurted out, "But I've no money."

"Don't worry, don't worry," he said, "You need that sandal more than I need the money."

He started working on the strap where it had snapped.

"You don't live around here, do you?" he asked in a friendly voice as he worked away. "You seem a little lost."

"I am lost," I murmured quietly, embarrassed. "I got on the wrong bus."

"Where do you want to go? I can tell you the bus route and show you to the bus stop."

I told him the address, and after a moment's hesitation I added, "But I lost my bus money."

He stopped in the midst of pulling a stitch taut and turned to look at me. Then he broke out laughing. I felt my face burn.

"You know, that's exactly what happened to me when I first came to the city," he said, going back to his stitching. "I got on the wrong bus, ended up completely lost and lost all my money. What luck, eh?"

He pulled the last stitch, tied a knot and cut off the thread.

"Here, try it. I think it's all good," he said passing the sandal to me. I put it on and walked a few steps; the sandal stayed intact.

"Great," he said with a satisfied nod and stood up. "Let's go then."

"Go? Go where?" I looked at him with confusion.

He laughed and patted my head. "Well, we need to get you home, don't we? We'll call your parents and see if they can pick you up. If not, I'll walk you to the bus station and buy you a ticket. Alright?"

For a moment I stared at him blankly, at a loss of words.

"What? What about your business?"
He waved his hand, "No worries. No one will come at this hour anyway."

I looked up at him and saw a warm glow in his eyes that I couldn't quite name back then. But now I know the right expression for that warmth radiating from the cobbler: it was compassion.

From time to time, I question the sincerity and selflessness of a compassionate deed. But in my moments of doubt, I always see the image of the cobbler in his cotton shift and the blue apron. His smiling black eyes look at me reminding me that once I have witnessed true compassion.

That one memory brings me courage and determination. Should I see a little girl one day, lost and lonely in another alley, I will not hesitate to play the cobbler.

Saviour

Art by Tian Yao

Saviour is a picture of a girl helping a little child in danger. Kindness to me means coming out of your "comfort zone" to help others. In this case the girl is leaving the safety of the sidewalk and helping a child off the street. The bus is coloured in dark shades to show the darkness of the danger, and the girl is in very light colours to show her compassion and kindness. When doing this project, I had to find out the true meaning of kindness and compassion. To me, it's putting the we before the me and helping others when they need it.

George An

Lost? Funabashi

Feathers filled the sky as a flock of pigeons took flight, and enthralled by them, I left the shopping bag and started to walk off towards an unfamiliar destination, chasing the birds. With the hot summer sun beating down, and the cicadas droning their endless screeches, I soon lost myself in the labyrinth of the streets of Tokyo. I had always been a spaced out, directionally challenged and distant person since I had been a toddler, so to me, getting lost in the large city of Funabashi-shi was no surprise. I was also an extremely introverted and shy person, so I didn't ask anyone I met along the way for directions to my home. Instead I trusted my five-year-old instincts and the theory of the "light at the end of the tunnel" and continued onwards along the streets, trying to find a familiar landmark. Unfortunately, the light at the end of the tunnel seemed to be misleading me and instead of making the situation better, I just got more scared and lost as I wandered along the surprisingly sparse streets.

Now, as I look back, I think to myself: "Wow, what a bad day that was." The morning had started out terribly and I should have been more careful. I had had a massive headache and an argument with my childhood friend that got me kicked out of class. And for lunch I had to eat *nattou* rice.

Never had my hometown of four years looked more frighteningly large and hostile in my whole life at Funabashi-shi. The bustling crowded city I had grown to like had suddenly become a ghost town in that hour of walking alone. Despairing, I sat down and tried to think of a way out, but with no new inspiration, I started to brood over the foolishness of what I had done previously. However, possibly because I didn't fully comprehend the situation, or more likely because I was never to be depressed for long, I brightened up and started to head

towards the far-away noise of the main streets, hoping to find some help there. Unluckily for me, I slipped and fell on a rock not three steps away. I ended up twisting my ankle that caused my right foot considerable pain when I tried to walk. Right around then, I almost lost patience with the world in general and just sat there in shock, hopeless and immobile.

I was resigned to the fate of those who get lost on deserted street corners (probably for no good reason, now that I look back), which was, of course, to be kidnapped by ghosts. But it was no netherworld being that approached me in the darkest moment of my five-year-old life, but a group of humans like me, or more precisely, a group of kids who were a few years older. These kids helped me get up and, after getting my address, helped me walk home. I could tell that they were already tired and I guessed that they were coming from a sports event that was held at a school nearby. But tired or not, they helped me home.

To those kids, I am very grateful. They helped me come back from a dark moment where I was confused, lost and depressed. The main point that left me with a deep impression was that they were complete strangers, people I may or may not ever meet again. And that to help me – someone they didn't know – must require a fair bit of caring and selflessness. They had recognized the distress I was in as I had been too embarrassed to ask for help for the indiscernible reason of a five-year-old. These kids taught me a great deal and I tried to be more sensitive and helpful around others after my experience. In the end, the "light at the end of the tunnel" was there, in the form of radiant kindness and caring for others.

Sriniti Sthapit

The People Next Door

Like most people I cannot recall many events that happened during the first few years of my life. However, there is one memory that stands out very vividly to me, even to this day. When I was four years old, my family moved to the Sudan. This country was so different from Nepal, my birthplace, that it might as well have been on Mars. At first I found the place so bizarre and foreign that I wondered if I would ever get used to a place like that. The Sudan was and is an extremely poor country where a cloud of poverty seems to be hovering above the people at all times. At that age, I didn't understand the realities of poverty, of not having the necessities of life. I could not understand nor imagine the misery and torture of extreme hunger and poverty.

The family next door was made up of a mom and her three children. They lived across the street from us in a place that shouldn't have been considered a home to anyone. There was literally only a roof over their heads to protect them from the elements which could be harsh at times. The intruding sandstorms were especially nasty, because the sand had the ability to invade every nook and cranny. Little did I know that the people next door, the people who did not have much, possessed the one thing the whole world could use a little more of: compassion.

One day my mother, my brother and I went grocery shopping while my dad was at work. When we came back home, my mom discovered that she had left the keys in the house and the main gate was locked. As a result, we couldn't get back inside. We had no way of getting into the house, so our only option was to wait for my father who would not be home until the evening. We stood outside in the stifling heat holding our many grocery bags, waiting as impatience slowly crept up on us. The three children across the street were playing outside. When they noticed us holding our grocery bags and waiting, they came to see what was going on. My mom explained what had happened and all three kids looked at us with eager eyes, ready to help. The oldest of the three pushed the garage door so that there was a small opening, barely enough for anyone to get through, or so we thought. Then he took my mom's grocery bags and slipped through the gap. The other two children followed his lead. They took our grocery bags inside for us and opened the gate that we could follow. When the three children slipped through the opening, I remember thinking, "Wow, they must be really skinny to fit through that small gap."

This might not have seemed like a big deal for the children, but we were very thankful that they came to our aid. We were strangers to them, but they saw that we needed help, and they simply acted. Thinking back on this memory now, I realize that this incident has impacted my life in many ways. I realize that to help others, one does not need to have money or material possessions, one just needs to have a big heart and the willingness to share with others. This simply goes to show that even small acts of compassion are just as great as big ones if it means making people feel better. If everyone did at least one thing, whether it is a small or big act of compassion toward others, it would make this world a much more beautiful place to live in.

Sorrow & Prayer

Art by Neil Johal

In my art piece, I portrayed a woman holding her hand over her heart, with another scene above, showing soldiers in combat. The woman is praying for the lives of the soldiers in battle, and, most importantly, her husband. The framed photo lying on the table next to her is supposed to be a photo of her husband. The image above with the soldiers is supposed to represent the circumstances of war, and what the woman is praying for. One man is hurt, with bandages all over, two men are dead, and one man is fighting back. Her eyes are closed, and her face almost expressionless, to show she is deep in thought and prayer. I smudged the edges to make the picture feel dark, but the woman is in a lighter place of the picture to show there's still hope (hence the light), and she's holding onto it.

Anisa Liria Adzijaj

Where Will I Go?

She sits down in the middle of the war's aftermath to take just one look at what used to be her home. It's obvious that malicious soldiers have been through the village, stealing, murdering and harming anyone they could. Her neighbourhood has been reduced to rubble. She looks over to her younger brother who is a heap on the dirt ground next to his mangled mother, weeping and tugging at her ruined dress. He appears to be weakening as blood seeps from his wounds and mixes with the earth. She watches him in a state of shock as his eyes roll back and his eyelids shut for the last time. They took her father and older brother. Not long after, she heard what sounded like three consecutive gunshots and then complete silence. She forces herself to stand up but her legs betray her and she collapses, ending up where she began. She's never felt so feeble. She's sick and tired of always being sick and tired. It's time to stop running and hiding: there's nothing to live for anymore. How quaint war is. What glory can be gained by taking the lives of others and watching them suffer? Who knew that a simple three-letter word could shake her once stable ground so ruthlessly? The image of war's repercussion has a permanent place burned into her mind dominating all other thoughts. She is so very, very alone and she's been denied a future. "What will happen to me?" she thinks. "Where will I go?"

A transitory war was fought in 1999 between NATO and Serbia, the chief remnant of the former Yugoslavia, over the status of the province of Kosovo. Over one million people fled the war in Kosovo and were sent to different parts of the world. I was ten years old when the war in Kosovo took place. I remember sitting in my living room turning on the television to watch cartoons, yet pausing when I came across a news channel. Images of distorted corpses flashed on the screen followed by images of grieving individuals, their eyes bleak and unresponsive. Watching all this left my heart torn at the seams. Not only were those people massacred, the survivors had nowhere to go. Or so I assumed. But Canada had opened its borders to refugees.

Ancient racial conflict between the Serbs and Kosovar-Albanians forced many people from their homes. The refugee outpour was the largest forced migration in Europe since WWII. Both my parents have roots in Kosovo and I admire them for helping the newcomers settle and try to rebuild their lives. My parents acted as translators. They communicated with refugees about their options and requirements. My brothers and I helped fundraise and collect new and used items to give to the immigrants. As more and more people arrived, I heard about the many wonderful actions Canadians took to make the transition less complicated for refugees. Hospitals took in as many people as they could to tend their injuries, both physical and mental. "Welcome houses" allowed entry to anyone needing a place to stay. And many Canadian citizens decided to sponsor families and offer them economical and moral support.

The intent was to help refugees recover from the trauma of war and adjust to life in a new location. Dislocation is a worldwide symptom of war and refugees of the world rely on the compassion and altruism of strangers.

I remember accompanying my dad to the Bridgeview Clinic. I watched as countless people flooded the hospital hallway, waiting patiently to speak to my dad and a doctor. They came and went, each one seemingly content with the brief exchange. Many of them showed a positive attitude in accepting help. These people were victims of ethnic cleansing, had had their homes burned, their family members killed and their lands strewn with mines, yet beaming smiles illuminated their faces.

With the conclusion of the open military unrest in Kosovo in June 1999, the majority of ethnic Albanians who had fled returned to their homes within a short time. I am certain that they would never forget the time spent in Canada and the kindness of its citizens. I think that this event opened the eyes of people around the world and made them realize how the empathy and selflessness of strangers can make one feel cherished and valuable.

Francisca Bradley

Boots & Birds

The girl was in a hurry. She was a Royal Canadian Sea Cadet, and she had an inspection that night. Every hair in her ultra-tight bun had to be in its place; every thread of her uniform was just where it should be.

Her feet thundered down the stairs as she ran to the ironing board to press the creases of her spotless trousers to stiff perfection. Steamed and starched, she grabbed them and sped to find her boots. They lay dusty beneath her bed. She blew away the dust and applied a few coats of polish, till they were as gleaming as a mirror. With every spot on her white-belt and gaiters abolished, she burst out of the house and carefully folded herself into the car. Her mother got into the driver's seat and shut the door. She then proceeded to lay her purse at her daughter's feet.

"Mum! Don't scuff my boots! I have an inspection tonight!"

"Okay Miss Snarky! Just remember who drives you everywhere!"

As the car started and backed out of the driveway, the girl checked herself in the mirror, adjusting her whitetop and smoothing her hair as they wound their way along the rural road. Ahead, out of the corner of her eye she noticed an oddly shaped rock sitting just beside the yellow line. As they whizzed by it, its feathers ruffled. Its feathers?

"Hey, Mum, There's a bird on the road!"

"You mean the dark thing by the yellow line? I thought that was a rock. It was a bird? Are you sure?"

"Yes! I saw its feathers ruffle as we drove by. It was sitting upright, it looks like it's in shock."

"It must have flown into somebody's windshield." There was a pause.

"We can't just leave it there, somebody will hit it!"

"You want to go back to save that bird?"

"Yes, I do! Hurry up please!" A large, black truck had just roared past, and the girl feared the worst. The girl's mother did a Mario Andretti turn and drove back the way she had come. The car stopped about 20 metres from the bird.

"That's as close as I can get without someone passing me and squishing it."

The girl threw the door open and was out of the car in a blink, whitetop askew, threads of hair coming loose and blowing in the gusts.

I shuddered as another huge wheel rushed past me and shook the ground. My feathers were ruffled from the drag winds of the ugly monsters that threatened to squash me flat. I wanted to fly away from these giant, smelly demons, but I couldn't make myself move. Yet another giant rocketed past, spitting rocks and sand that stung my eyes and caused me great agony. My head and neck were aching so much. I was dizzy and could barely see. Suddenly, I was aware of a girl all dressed in black with a strange white hat. I resigned myself to the worst; I was about ready to die. I fluffed my feathers and buried my neck in them, shivering from the cold and the shock. Two very large, shiny shoes stopped about a foot from the tip of my beak. I raised my head and saw that the girl was bending over me and extending her hands. She eased me onto her hand and formed a gentle cup with the other. I warbled and sang appealingly at her. I should have been scared, but I just knew this girl meant no harm.

My tiny talons clung to a finger and I buried myself in her warm, protective palm. She proceeded to move off the road, moving gently so as to cause me no great discomfort, dodging angry vehicles.

Through an opening in her palm, I could see the plain, unobstructed sky change to trees and bushes. The girl made her way down a steep embankment and into some long thistles and grass. Here, she knelt and flattened and formed a little hollow in which she placed me, making sure I would not be caught up if I flew out.

I let go of her finger with some reluctance, not wanting to give up the warmth and protectiveness. I settled down into the grass and warbled another song for her. The girl smiled at me. She stood up slowly and backed away, still stooped over, watching me. Then she turned, climbed up the embankment and was gone.

The girl moved quickly across the road and back to the car. Her heart ached to stay with the little creature and be sure that he was alright but, no, she must leave and get to school; she was already late. She looked down at the seeds and grass stuck to her pants, the mud and scratches on her boots. She tried to stuff her hair back under her hat. The car ate up the miles into town, and when they finally reached the school, the girl paused only to kiss her mother goodbye and was gone.

"Why are you so late, PO?" inquired one of her officers.

"I stopped to save a bird, Sir," she replied, "He was sitting on the yellow line and I stopped to make sure he was safe."

"A bird, PO?"

"Yes, Sir."

He chuckled, "Now there's a real Sea Cadet in action. Fall in."

"Yes, Sir!"

Later, the girl recounted the events to her friends.

"Good for you, PO," some of them said.

"Awesome, Bradley," noted one of her seniors. Someone snickered, "I would have just driven over it. You're a softie."

There was a silence as everyone in the room was stilled by the awkwardness. The girl realized that not everyone had enough empathy to see through the eyes of a small, helpless creature in need.

"But some of us do," she thought to herself, "and that is the saving grace."

Art by Jeffrey King

Photo by Karen San

Laura Ritland

Breaking the Silence

The air is dusty during the hot muggy school recess. The sun burns in the sky like an angry yellow eye bleaching the yellow lines that mark the basketball court.

I sit in the shadow under the eves of the school roof, dust swirling around me as I shift from crouching to sitting. Knobbly, elephant-skin knees protrude from my pink shorts and one fine-lined scar runs up my leg like a stitch in the fabric of my skin. I want to pick at it, but know that it will bleed.

The wall that my back is resting against is made of stucco painted orange. Straws and wrappers litter the base, a garbage bin sits to my right. There are little dents in the orange paint where the white base is revealed, little dents like tooth marks.

I am dimly aware of the children around me. I can hear their shrieks and skipping rope chants, and I can feel a breeze when they push past me, hot and sweaty. Carefully I look up at the playground with its shiny

equipment. I want to play. I desperately want to be among those children clanging on the slide, swinging on the monkey bars, screaming as they chase one another. I want to be able to stand up and move, and be part of the crowd – doesn't everyone?

But the silence around me will not be broken. The joyous sounds of the children surround me, drowning me in their happiness. I'm supposed to go and play, but I can't. I will not.

Thud.

A soccer ball bounces off the side of the stucco wall. I stay very still, hoping that whoever kicked it will go away.

Thud.

I turn and curl myself into a small ball, press my nose into my knees and stare down at the skin now stretched smoothly across them. Armadillos do this, to protect themselves with their hard bony skin, and maybe I can

Photo by Michelle Tsang

too. I can hear laughter and chatter as the ball bounces over and over again into the wall.

Thud.

The ball slams into my back and I feel my breath being expelled from me. I want to turn around and look, but my limbs feel like stone. If I just ignore them maybe they'll go away. Maybe they've seen me and will go and play somewhere else.

I feel a hand tap on my shoulder and peek out of the corner of my eye, through my hair, up into a boy's red face. He has too many freckles.

"Hey, can you go and sit somewhere else? We're trying to play a game here," he says impatiently.

I stand up and walk away without looking back, my throat tight.

This day is like yesterday, and the day before that, and the day before that. I don't want to think that tomorrow will be like this. I would prefer to think tomorrow I will have a hundred friends to play a million games with skipping ropes, soccer balls, on slides and monkey bars. I would prefer to think that.

But it's hard to imagine.

I am passing the windows and I can see the scene reflected in the black mirrors, illuminated by the harsh sunlight. Behind me, the boys are kicking the brown soccer ball, the girls are playing hopscotch, other children play tag. I can see myself too, and I notice my eyes – wide, dark and frightened, and suddenly they scare me with their desperation.

Five years later in a different school, on a different playground, I come across the same wide eyes – in another face. I feel a tremble run down my spine as recognize the expression. It is a dusty day, with the sun glaring down without mercy and I remember the silence. And the stucco and the thud of the soccer ball.

Those eyes. They are staring at me from a small round face, fringed by dark hair. He is so small, wearing jeans with the knees rubbed to white. He sits in the shade with his back against the white-washed wall, alone. Around us, children shriek.

I could just leave the boy sitting there and hope someone will deal with him. I could just turn my back and ignore him like everyone else. I could think he deserved to suffer as I did, out of spite.

But I don't. And to this day I wonder – if I hadn't suffered the silence myself, would I understand him?

"Hey," I say softly to the boy, "You want to play?" Silence. Then slowly, he nods.

Shania Kelly
Walking Home

As I walk, I think about an event that happened years ago, but is still affecting my life. It was not some ordinary kindness done just because people were watching. No, it was more than that. It was an ordinary kindness made extraordinary by the way it was performed. I was the only one to see, and the person did not see me. It was the most amazing thing I had ever seen. It was not just some person helping someone up off the ground, it was someone guiding me, and showing me the way to true happiness; happiness that is gained from helping others, happiness that is gained by being kind. There is no better method, no better way.

Here is the story: I was walking home from school, and when I was walking past an alley I noticed someone being bullied. I did nothing; I thought there was nothing I could do. Someone else was walking past; she stopped and said, "Why are you picking on this young lady?" She said it with such force, such anger, that the bullies ran away. She offered the girl a hand, and she took it gratefully, "Thank you so much, I thought I was doomed," she said, and she looked so thankful, so glad that this person had come. "Well I couldn't just leave you there with all the bullies. Why, they ought to be ashamed of themselves!" She spoke, emphasizing the last bit of the sentence. Before she left she made sure the girl was all right. Then she walked away slowly looking back often, until she reached the corner, when she looked back one last time before turning.

And as the girl walked away, I came out of my hiding spot and began to walk home. I knew that after seeing that compassion, I could not just walk away from a scene like that ever again, without stopping to help. I realized that I had always wanted to be kind, but I did not believe myself brave enough to step in. Now I realized that it does not matter, that it is okay as long as your intentions are good, that it is okay to be scared, that you do not have to be courageous. I knew there was no way out of being kind now, I wanted to prove that I was kind.

The next day I saw the same girl in the same situation, and did I stop? Yes, I walked straight in and said, "I don't think this is quite fair, after all, doesn't this happen every day? And I don't think she enjoys this treatment. Do you think she does?" I spoke sharply to them, and I didn't let them answer before I helped the girl up, and we started to walk away.

I did this every day, until they stopped bugging her, and by then we were best friends.

And now even as I grow older, I tell everyone I can about how seeing an act of kindness changed my life forever. I want to be a teacher and when I reach that goal, at every opportunity I will give my students examples of compassion and kindness. I will try to do everything I can to teach others to be kind. I figure that if people get along better, and are kinder towards each other, there'll be no World War III. If you get the chance to influence the next generation, then influence it for the better, not for the worse. Help them to grow to be better people; don't teach them the cruel ways of fools. This will forever and always be my motto, all because of one little act of kindness. This story shows you that kindness always brings good things, sometimes friendship. But mostly it is enough to know that you are a good person, a kind person, someone people can count on. This is usually reward enough.

Jackie Nattress

Dangerous Dive

One scorching hot summer day, my friend Rachel and I were hanging out inside. We were desperate to go for a swim, so we set off for Pebbly Beach. As Rachel and I were walking down the road, we bumped into our friends Maia and Peter who were also heading to Pebbly Beach. We saw that Peter had his arm in a cast and asked him what had happened. He answered that he had been riding his new bike when he had fallen off and broken his arm.

As soon as we got to Pebbly Beach, Rachel, Maia and I ran into the water. The water was nice and cool and, oh, so refreshing. We decided to swim out to the raft and play. When we reached the raft, we looked back towards the beach and saw Peter sitting on his towel playing with rocks. Peter had the loneliest expression on his face. Looking at Peter and seeing his sad expression made me feel so bad. I remembered how we had rushed into the water to swim when we got to the beach. None of us had remembered that Peter couldn't swim by himself. Rachel, Maia and I swam back to the shore to help Peter. As soon as we got there, we thought it would be a good idea to bring my family's big windsurfing board along, just in case. After getting the board into the water, we helped Peter get on. Peter was really excited and happy that he was finally going to have a chance to swim.

I swam pulling the board bearing Peter out to the raft. There we asked Peter what he wanted to do. He replied that he wanted to try swimming out to the old boat *Black Eyes* that we called a pirate ship. We weren't sure if Peter would be able to make it with his broken arm, so we refused. But Peter kept pleading with us and saying: "Please, you could help me do it." So we decided that we would all go out together. Once we reached the boat, we

had to find a way up. We saw a rope that hung about a foot under water, we grabbed it and Rachel climbed up to the boat using the rope to heave herself up. This was too hard for Peter. So Maia and I tried to think of another way. I saw that the boat had round windows so we helped Peter put his feet on the ridge that was by the window. Then all Peter had to do was grab Rachel's hand so she could hoist him up. When Maia and I finished climbing up, we all explored the boat. We found lots of neat things including a rusty weird-shaped knife, a seagull skull, an old glass jar and a really big anchor.

Rachel, Maia and I decided to jump from the side into the water. We weren't too sure, because it looked really scary. Once we had jumped, we climbed back on. Peter was really jealous that he couldn't do what we did. When we weren't looking, he jumped off the side of the boat. I turned around and all I saw was Peter's arms. I felt so scared. Then I ran and looked over the side of the boat and saw Peter crying and trying to stay above water.

I quickly jumped in and he clutched my shoulder. When Peter grabbed me, I could feel the tension from Peter's arms run through my body, I could hear him breathing heavily. I swam as fast as I could. It was incredibly hard, because Peter was on my back. I had to struggle to keep my head above water. I was so scared that I was going to sink or my arms and legs would get tired. But then Maia and Rachel were right behind me on the surfboard, so we could help Peter get on. As soon as we got safely to the shore, his mom came to get him. The expression on Peter's face was incredible, he just looked at me and smiled with gratitude and relief. I felt exhausted, but happy that we had managed to get him back safely.

Sara Lim

Two's Better Than One

Cold dust
Shivers through the streets
Pulling at my hat and coat
My fingers shrivel back into their
sleeves
Gloveless, regretful
I skid across hard shimmering concrete
Nearly lose balance in
Two-inch heels

I need shelter
A snail crosses my path
Hunched over, struggling against the
wind
A bulging pack on his back
I watch his muted meandering
But see an alley
Dark foreboding
I lean against a sticky wall
Thankful for protection

Then I hear mewling
I follow it
A shoebox
I lift the top off
Six bony grime kittens
Five rotting dead
Hollow eyes

Plump white globs of worm
Squirming inside
Bitter decay up my nostrils
I cough, stepping away
Intent on leaving

Then I hear the mewling again.
I pause, and watch the poor creature
Barely alive
Attempts to climb out the shoebox
His matted legs
Violent shake
His eyes a milky film
He falls a dull thud
A thunder crash
To his tiny ears

I am still
The kitten tries again
His head is bumpy
One ear
Missing fur
Both paws over the edge of the box
Moving like an hourglass
Falling one grain of sand at a time
His stringy muscles straining
He starts to shake again
My heart moans

I kneel down
Cradling his whole body
In my right palm
He sneezes
Thick yellow, sour-smelling mucous
From his nose
I hold him closer still
Against my shivering body
I gaze down at him
Three fat snails crawling up
His back
He smells of mouldy milk vomit
His every movement
Quivers

I fall in love with him.

I look back up to keep
My tears from hitting him
I slip off my heels
Bare feet
Better traction
I run down the street
Yelling for someone

Fleeing Cat

Photo by Shaylene Charleson

The cat is running so fast, it looks like it has a deep fear of people, maybe because of a bad experience. This cat needs to be cared for and loved so it can stop being so scared. Showing the cat love and compassion will help it lose its fear of people.

Hafiz Kassam

Sharing the Burden

Imagine, for a moment, walking through a community where paved streets are a novelty, where electricity is never assured and where the police create more chaos than order. Now imagine walking through a Brazilian *favela* trying to meet people who call this place home, all the while looking for a small resemblance to a regular Canadian neighbourhood. You feel like you can smell success when you find a group of boys huddled together, mulling over some new toy. Now imagine the shock of finding that it is not a toy at all, but a shiny new pistol given to these prospective *soldados* by the leader of the local drug faction.

These boys are high on glue, have no formal education and are being recruited into the drug trade, yet they are smiling. They are smiling because for one of the few times in their short lives, a complete stranger is trying to communicate with them in a mixture of broken Portuguese and hand gestures. A stranger is listening to them and shows a genuine interest in their lives.

Compassion is a basic idea. It is a concept that cannot be assigned a numeric value. It can only be evaluated by the people who are sharing it. Compassion comes in many forms and is often misunderstood. A major flaw in the mentality of North American students, particularly from privileged backgrounds, is the misconception of what it is to help and show compassion to others. Far too often, students in service clubs and global awareness societies operate under the impression that issues, of which they only have superficial knowledge, can be solved by raising enough money or by logging extra volunteer hours. They fail to realize that in order to genuinely help, a person must understand the needs of the people, he or she is trying to support. They must take the time to educate themselves about the situation and become culturally grounded in that certain community in order to find its fundamental problems, not just the most visible ones. They fail to realize that the greatest synonym of compassion is not change but understanding.

I am often angered by organizations who insist that they understand the issue, yet operate under the pretense that the origin of the others' problems lie in a lack of structure that are integral to their own communities. History has shown – from the missionaries in First Nation communities to the use of financial aid in developing countries – that imposing a foreign structure, even with good intentions, can have devastating effects on a community. It is groups that actively engage with the problems of a community, share its burden and treat the foreign problems as their own, that can have a positive impact.

It is frustrating to witness the misguided application of compassion in North America and to see that it is not often questioned. Having spent time with people who depend on others, from communities in Brazil to Vancouver, I have seen the lack of understanding in the world and the pain of being patronized in one's own community. It is my hope that through education initiatives, the genuine notion of compassion will begin to resurface and people will begin to make effective changes and positive connections throughout the world.

Rebecca Reardon

Leaving Peru

Compassion is the deep feeling of sadness and smpathy toward others who are surrounded by pain and misfortune, and a strong desire and will to alleviate that suffering.

In February of 2008, I had the opportunity, with three other students, to travel to Peru to aid those who were affected by the earthquake that happened in August of 2007, and to help those less fortunate than I. This was a life-changing experience for me, because I had never done anything this big before. I had volunteered at soup kitchens here. But to travel half-way around the world to help others was a new experience and an unbelievable feeling.

As soon as we arrived in Peru, we were on our way to a town on the coast called Chin Cha. This town was one of the many places that had been greatly affected by the earthquake. While we were traveling to Chin Cha, we saw beautiful scenery and landscape, but the houses and conditions people lived in were horrific. Many people were living in box-shaped huts, no bigger than a single room. These shanty homes were scattered throughout the desert landscape.

Seeing something as heartbreaking as this on television, reading about it or hearing about it is one thing, but actually being there and witnessing what is going on gave me a completely different perception. As I watched this shocking scene pass by, I felt so sad inside. I also had a load of guilt on my shoulders because I realized how spoiled and greedy we are in our part of the world; we live a life of luxury. I was so glad to be in Peru. It made me feel proud and good inside that I was going to help.

When we arrived in Chin Cha, the first thing we noticed was that many of the buildings had collapsed and were in ruins because of the earthquake. It was hard to take in, but we knew we were here to help. We immediately went to work delivering the construction materials necessary to build small community centres to six building sites throughout the town. This was a lot of work, but in the end, it was very rewarding.

Building the community centre had to be the most memorable time of the entire trip for me. While we were working there the people who lived in the surrounding area came out to help us. This was a very touching experience. Among the people coming to see us was a little girl who was about six years old. She and I bonded as soon as we met. She took me around everywhere she went and I instantly fell in love with her. As day turned into night we had accomplished what we had come to do and the time to part had arrived.

Art by Tina Yuan

This was a very difficult moment for me because as everyone thanked us, the little girl ran up and jumped into my arms. At that moment everything around me just disappeared and all kinds of feelings accumulated inside me. The meaning and feeling of compassion was overwhelming. I didn't want to leave. I knew that I wanted to stay and continue to help these people who were surrounded by disaster and misfortune.

Leaving Peru was a hard thing to do. But I knew that we had made a positive impact in many people's lives. And I am glad and proud that I had the opportunity to be a part of it. My trip to Peru was an experience of a life time and I know that in the future I will participate in additional service projects and acts of compassion around the world as well as here, at home.

Art by Tessa Goldie

For the compassion project, I drew a girl in a green, happy and peaceful world looking into a well. She does not see her own reflection in the water, but many other faces of children in a poverty-stricken part of the world. The girl has her hands out to show she wants to help. The tear dripping down her face shows that she is sad for them. This girl has compassion and she wants to make a difference. On the far right side in the well is a boy who is smiling, while the rest of the children are sad or crying. I wanted to show that one child knows the girl cares and that his life will change one day – he has hope.

Annie Van

Relief

You see two doors.
Door number one and door number two
Door number one has a sign on it.
The sign says, "door of suffering."

You reach for the knob.
A chilling sensation travels up your arm
Through your body
Into your head.
You see

A young boy with a bloated belly.
Tears streaming down his cheek.
Surrounded by the sweltering heat.

You reach for his arm.
You touch nothing
There was nothing
It's a mirage.
Yet your mind is full of emotions.

You let go of the doorknob and take a step back.
Door number two has a sign on it.
The sign says, "door of relief."

You reach for the knob.
A warm sensation runs up your arm
Through your body
Into your head.
The doorknob lets out a quiet squeak as you turn it.
You see

A young boy with a bloated belly.
Tears streaming down his cheek.
Surrounded by the sweltering heat.

You reach for his arm.
You touch his delicate skin.
The young boy wipes away a tear and smiles.

Kiara Anderson
Loading Trucks

My great-uncle, Doctor A. Simone, has been doing remarkable things for many years. His mind is always set on helping other people. And I admire him.

Last summer while I was in Toronto visiting my family, my uncle and I went to a huge warehouse where big trucks are loaded full of clothes, food, drinks, walking sticks, wheelchairs, school supplies and many other things. My uncle has been bringing high school students there to contribute their efforts to the working site. Not only does he encourage other people to help, he often travels to developing countries himself to deliver the food. He makes sure that all the things that have been collected reach their destination.

The first thing I noticed when I arrived at the warehouse, were the people. There were many different kinds of people, some able-bodied, some with disabilities. Many people from different racial backgrounds were working together to help the less fortunate. For about two hours I loaded trucks with a variety of things. As I worked I could picture the kids receiving these goods. I imagined them going crazy over the little things such as food and school supplies, things I take for granted every day.

On the ride home I thought about what I had just done. It made me feel good that I helped someone far away who had less than me. Then I thought about my uncle. He has done this for many years, helping people all over the world. And all I did was pack a few trucks for two hours. They say that everything you do helps, and it does.

I just wish there were more people like my uncle. No, I wish that everyone was like him.

Art by Roos Schut

To me compassion means feeling empathy for others and wanting to help. Many people in the Western world want to help children in developing nations. The blue iris represents the Western World. The eye is crying – symbolizing compassion as well as rain. The rain falls into the woven basket of the African girl, thus filling it up as she walks along. I chose to draw a girl because in developing nations girls are often not well-educated. The education of girls plays a vital part in solving poverty. The girl walks on a never-ending path because poverty seems to be an ongoing problem. The mountains represent freedom. And the path does lead to freedom – freedom from poverty and into a new life. I want people to understand that there is a solution to poverty and we will learn what that is during our journey.

Hedy Chan
Dreaming of Reality

Just yesterday I was thinking…
What if the stars in the sky;
Meters, miles, and kilometers away.
Really weren't that far.
But can be reached with a stretch of an arm.
But as easy as that sounds
Even this stretch takes effort and time.

This stretch is the build up to that star, the destination.
Your Dream.
This stretch holds the experience you have gathered
Both ups and downs
This stretch is the flower that has bloomed
From a tiny seed to a full grown flower
This stretch holds what may only have meaning to you
And no one else.

All this is your dream
What you want to happen
What you had envisioned yourself doing
So you took action
And took the step, to reach out and grab your dream
No, it is now the reality you have achieved using your own hands.